The Battle Behind the Sword

The Battle Behind the Sword

My Struggles, My Truth

Lady Linda Jenise

Williams and King Publishers

Copyright 2018.

All rights reserved. No part of this publication may be reproduced, stored in a retrieval system, or transmitted in any way by any means electronic, mechanical, photocopy, recorded or otherwise without the prior permission of the copyright holder, except by reviewer who may quote brief passages in a review to be printed in magazine, newspaper or radio/TV announcement, as provided by USA copyright law. The author and the publisher will not be held responsible for errors within the manuscript.

Williams and King Publishers
306 Ocoee Apopka Rd. #5
Ocoee, FL 34761

Orlando, Florida
ISBN: 978-0-9998406-3-4

Printed in the USA

For he is the minister of God to thee for good. But if thou do that which is evil, be afraid; for he bares not the sword in vain: for he is the minister of God, a revenger to execute wrath upon him that doeth EVIL" (Romans 13:4).

Table of Contents

CHAPTER ONE 1
    REMINISCING

CHAPTER TWO 9
    SHE WAS STILL MY MOTHER

CHAPTER THREE 19
    MY HOUSE WAS NOT A HOME

CHAPTER FOUR 27
    THE DAY MOMMA LEFT ME

CHAPTER FIVE 41
    NOBODY'S LITTLE GIRL

CHAPTER SIX 55
    BROKEN

CHAPTER SEVEN 65
    RAGING STORMS

CHAPTER EIGHT 77
  NO STRENGTH TO FIGHT

CHAPTER NINE 93
  THIS IS TOO MUCH GOD

CHAPTER TEN 109
  IT'S ALL GOOD

CHAPTER 11 121
  NEVERTHELESS – NOT MY WILL
  BUT THY WILL BE DONE

CHAPTER TWELVE 143
  PICKING UP THE PIECES OF MY HEART

EXCERPTS FROM MY JOURNAL

Introduction

"For the Son of man is come to seek and to save that which was lost," (Luke 19:10)

Let me start off by saying what ministry is and what ministry is not. Ministry is not this glamorous life that many portray it to be. If the truth is told, true ministry is quite the opposite. True ministry requires a lot of suffering, a lot of studying, and a lot of self-discipline, and a whole lot of prayer. When you accept the "call of God," the truth is, your life is no longer yours. When you are in ministry that is truly for God, then your very steps are ordered by Him. In order to be in true ministry, God has to position His people to be able to hear His voice when He speaks to them, and the only way to hear Gods voice is to learn His Word.

Ministry is not a career move to make one rich, famous, or to be liked and well known. I have seen so many preachers that are *pimping* the gospel for their own benefit. According to the Bible, the gospel is used to seek and save that which is lost. It is not about putting together a message, getting a lot of members and living the high life off of the people's money. True ministry is not even behind a pulpit. Paul and the Apostles' ministry was out in the streets, preaching to the lost. They were out of their comfort zones, out ministering and suffering for the cause of Christ.

The flip side of ministry is that all clergymen are not after their members' money, nor are they seeking fame. There are some ministers that are truly concerned about the well-being of the souls. Don't get me wrong, I am not against ministers having money, and I am not against people giving to the church from where they eat. The Bible teaches us to give and to be cheerful about giving. The Bible also says that the men of God are due double honor. If you want to bless your leader, then you do whatever God has laid on your heart to do; it is your money.

However, I am against those ministers that demand to be taken care of and demand to be treated like royalty from the church. These minsters are the "glory snatchers." They want the glory all to themselves and God is nowhere to be found. It's all about them, and what they have done, and who they are. Can we please put Jesus back in the church? Can we give God His glory back? It's His anyway, whether you give it to Him or not. "For of Him, and through Him, and to Him are all things: to whom be GLORY forever. Amen" (Romans 11:36). Yep, the GLORY BELONGS TO GOD! It is in Him that we live, breathe, move and have our being. It doesn't take a genius to figure out that we are nothing without HIM!

I have been in several church settings where the ministers look like clowns in a circus. This had literally made me sick to my stomach especially when I looked around at the congregation and I saw the people of God were hurting and the leaders were not concerned at all. I've been in church services where the people in the congregation are struggling to make ends meet financially, doing the best they could to be all that God has called them to be. These people were paying their tithes faithfully; they were there every time the doors of the church opened, but as members, they were not able to get any help from the church.

I have a problem with that, and I am sure that God does too. Then the pastor of the church would get up and start talking about his house, how many bedrooms it has, what kind of car he drives and how much money he has. This is to every minister that is preaching the Gospel deceitfully just for a profit. I want to serve you notice, that God is going to come see you, sir or ma'am. Also, don't think for one minute that spiritual people cannot discern your spirit and see through your manipulation tactics. Just because no one ever says anything to you, doesn't mean they don't know, and that you are getting over. The Bible says, "That which is done in the dark shall also be brought to the light." God never said whose light He was going to bring it too. So yes, the person sitting next to you may know you aren't any good and that you are using the Gospel for your benefit. Oh, and they also know that *you* called yourself into the ministry.

At an early age, having the gift of spiritual discernment, I learned that God is real. Now I don't claim to know the entire Bible, but I do know when things are not of God. Many things we know are not of God, yet we continue to let them fly in the church; God will judge. Some of the music and dances I see in the church, should bring shame to the house of God. The leaders don't say anything. They just let it fly because they want those seats filled, and the tithes and offerings. They want the people to make them look good, but the truth be told, for those that are truly spiritual our hearts cry out for the people and as for the leaders, "Be not deceived; God is not mocked: for whatsoever a man soweth, that shall he also reap" (Galatians 6:7).

Now let me talk about myself and ministry. When I am ministering, preaching, teaching or praying, or whatever it is that God is calling for me to do at that moment, the ministry being manifested. However, you don't see the preparation of the ministry, or the making of this ministry with which God has entrusted me. You don't see the loneliness, the late-night tears that I cried, or the betrayal that I have encountered. You don't see the struggles that I have endured, all you see is the outward ministry as you hear the message. Yes, it sounds good, it looks good, and it looks like fun, but you don't know what went on behind the scenes.

Ministry is not up sweating and giving a good message. Nor is ministry making people shout and speak in tongues, but true ministry is allowing God to take you to the deepest part of the valley, and then rely on only Him to bring you out. Sometimes while you are in the valley, many times God will allow you to go through a "no season." A "no season" is a season where no matter where you turn for help, the answer is "No." God has allowed the people that would normally help you, reject your cries. It is because God wants you to depend solely on Him to bring you up out of the valley.

Ministry is staying in the fight and not giving up, not giving in, and not giving out. Ministry is trusting God no matter where He leads you. Whether He leads you around the Red Sea, or through it - whichever way, He becomes your source. He becomes your go-to person while you are in the valley, or while you are in trouble. The valley is much like the belly of the whale, because you can't go up, and you can't go down - all you can do is cry out to Him from the depths of your soul, just as Jonah did, and yes, it feels like pure torment. "And said, I cried by reason of mine affliction unto the LORD, and He heard me; out of the belly of hell cried I, and Thou heardest my voice. For Thou hadst cast me into the deep, in the midst of the seas; and the floods compassed me about: all thy billows and Thy waves passed over me. Then I said, I am cast out of Thy sight, yet I will look again toward Thy holy temple." (Jonah 2: 2-4).

The valley experience for ministry is not a one-time trip, but it is several trips to the valley, and each trip the valley gets deeper and deeper, darker and darker, lonelier and lonelier. I have found that true ministers of God are those that never wanted to preach in the first place. Those are the ones that God tells them to go left, and they go right. They are the ones who run, and run, and run, and run until God just takes them through so much darkness that they have no other choice but to surrender. After all, He chose you; you didn't choose Him. I was one of those ministers and the truth is, in the end, God gets His way.

Christians need to understand that whenever we see a minister who is anxious to get behind the pulpit just to deliver a message, or if he demands that you address him by his title, or he has that prideful and haughty spirit, RUN!! Those ministers usually don't want to talk about God, but they want to talk about their ministry, what they are doing to their building, how many members they have, or how much they get paid in salary. They want to talk about stuff that doesn't even matter; again, I say, RUN!! Be aware of those ministers that don't care anything about our souls, but all they want is to be our headship to give from our wallets. Those types of ministers preach the truth. They are very biblically knowledgeable, but they are very deceitful, cunning and crafty when preaching the Word of God. In this hour we must make sure that we are in tune with God so that we are not deceived by this cunning spirit.

Also, in today's church we have the manipulative master

ministers. These are the ministers that tell the church what they want to hear and who will preach the things that will tickle the ear of the people. They will show you a lot of concern and give the impression that they really do care. They will begin to say things about other ministers and ministries that they see wrong. Don't be deceived, this is a tactic that they use just to make it seem like their ministry have everything together. The truth is they just want you to be a part of their congregation so that it can seem like everyone else's gospel is of non-effect. These ministers go to many different programs with one purpose in mind, and that is to scope out everything wrong with the service, the message, the singing, or even the door so that they can have more ammunition to prove their point. Oh, and they have scriptures to back them up; again, RUN!!

Pay attention to preachers that are quick to run to the pulpit to deliver a word. Children of God, please don't be caught up in the hype. These types of preachers normally preach messages to get you hyped-up, so that you can give them your money; do not be deceived by this. They are either not sent, not ready, or have other motives which are normally their own motives. The Bible says, "This people draweth nigh to me with their mouth and honoreth me with their lips, but their heart is far from me. But in do they worship me, teaching for doctrines the commandments of men" (Matthew 15: 8-9).

I just want people to beware of the ministers of the gospel in today's time. James 1:27 says, "Pure religion and undefiled before God and the Father is this, to visit the fatherless and widows in their affliction and to keep himself unspotted from the world." Whew, that scripture will preach just by itself.

How many ministers are doing what the scripture has instructed us to do? A lot of preachers don't even visit the sick and the shut-ins anymore. I saw this act of kindness demonstrated more in the country that I did in the city. As a matter of fact, I don't even know if the citified preachers even know this scripture exist; too funny! Enough of my venting about ministers, pastors, preachers, ministers, prophets, or whatever they want to be called.

I knew that God had called me to the ministry at an early age. I was probably around thirteen or fourteen years old. Let me point out something; just because you said "yes" to ministry work does not mean that you are ready for battle. For example, just because I go to Bible study and learn one or two scriptures does not mean that I am ready to preach a sermon. We must be tried by the fire. God has to know that He can trust us with trouble, pain, and with the deepest darkest secrets of His people. He needs to know that He can trust us with money as well. Can He trust you to be a good steward? Then there is one question that can make or break you in ministry. That question is, "Can God trust you with betrayal?"

The reason this question stands out is that betrayal produces many kinds of emotions. Many people operate out of emotions, or their feelings. This is "no-go" for ministry. Betrayal also produces a pain that causes a spirit of vengeance. God must know that He can trust us while we are in the fire. What that means is when betrayal comes and the fire is turned up, will we seek Him, will we quit, or will we seek revenge? Now, deciding to quit one day and seek Him the next does not mean that we gave up. That scenario simply means that we were emotional and speaking in that way.

I told God many times, "I quit! If this is ministry, I'm good. You can miss me with this madness! You can keep your ministry work. God, find somebody else!" That, by itself, is another book, however, you will read some of the times when I said, "I'm done," and then got back up, back in my Bible, and was right back at church, early Sunday morning. I believe it's safe to say that God has a spiritual hold on me that cannot be destroyed by the troubles of life. Oh, don't get me wrong, life can hurt me, but it can't destroy me; because I stand on the promises of God. The Bible says, "He that dwelleth in the secret place of the most High shall abide under the shadow of the Almighty. I will say of the Lord, He is my refuge and my fortress: my God; in him will I trust" (Psalms 91).

When dealing with ministry, we first must recognize the call of ministry that has been placed on our lives. We must understand that ministry is a call that God gives, not man. Let me repeat that statement. Ministry is a call that God gives, not man. It doesn't matter if a pastor, preacher, bishop, or whoever says, "I need you to be a minister." You had better respond, "God bless, but I must seek the Lord on that one." Or, if you know God has not called you into ministry, let them know respectfully that God has not called you to ministry. Don't fall into the hype and take up a spiritual position that God did not authorize.

When reading about John the Baptist, we find that he understood his role in ministry. He preached, "Repent, for the Kingdom of heaven is at hand." John understood that he was not Jesus. He also let the people know that he was not Jesus and that He would come after (whose shoelaces he was not worthy to untie). In those days, to stoop down and loosen the sandals was a common act of a slave stooping down to his master with all humility and respect. Although John was on the front line, and he could have easily tried to snatch the glory for himself, but instead he esteemed Jesus higher than himself and displayed his true character which was humility.

John then continued to display his character and to let people know that he understood his purpose. Even when the busybodies tried to be a distraction, he remained focused on his purpose. When the people came to John and told him that there were others who were following Jesus, he said, "I must decrease so that Jesus can increase." This statement alone suggests that John was not in it for himself, but he was in it for the promoting of the Kingdom.

When Jesus came on the scene, John still understood his assignment. He did not let people boost him into becoming something that he knew that he was not called to do. He understood that he was not the Messiah, that person was Jesus. The lesson that we all can learn from John is, do not allow people to fill our heads with foolishness, boost our ego, and hype us up into doing something that we know God has not called us to do.

Let me very clear in what I am saying. In some cases, God may have been tugging on us to do a specific assignment for the Kingdom, whether it be a minister, a praise and worship leader, or a deacon. Sometimes He will send someone to confirm what He had already put in our spirit.

I have seen what happens to many people who let a "man" call them into the ministry and not God. According to the Bible, God says, "Whom I've called, I have qualified." This is why you see so many preachers whose ministry is of non-effect because they are operating in a calling that was not authorized by God. Let's just be truthful about the whole matter: some people have called themselves into ministry.

I've heard some preachers who have called themselves into ministry. They can really preach too, but the preaching is entertaining and there is no anointing. If the anointing was present in the preacher himself, then it would change him as a man of God. Anytime someone can preach a good fiery message, and still go back out sinning without any conviction, that person is an entertainer. The Word clearly says that gifts come without repentance. Meaning, one does not have to repent and be saved to have a gift to minister. It is just the same as one does not have to be saved to be able to play an instrument.

Those gifts are given by God Himself, and He assigns them to whomever He chooses. But woe to the person who preaches the gospel of Jesus Christ without any intent to live a life that aligns with His Word. God's wrath comes quickly!

I was so excited about ministering. I remember one day sitting in my bedroom watching a gospel channel on my black and white television, filled with enthusiasm. I didn't know at the time, but the Holy Spirit had caused a shaking in my spirit. He (the Holy Spirit) began to minister to me all that night. I was so happy to know that I was going to die and meet Jesus, and all the apostles, and prophets. My mother was there to witness this excitement. She came running in my bedroom because I was jumping up and down on the bed and screaming because I was so happy. She said, "What is wrong with you?" I answered, "I'm going to heaven and I am going to meet Jesus, and He has called me into the ministry, and I am so excited!" She looked at me and said, "That's good baby, but you are going to meet Jesus sooner than you think if you don't stop jumping in that bed."

I can look back on it now and laugh, but it wasn't funny then. It must have been the Spirit that took over me because if I had been in my right mind there was no way that I would have had a conversation with my mother, all while jumping on the bed.

If you knew my mother, then you would know that would have been suicide.

The truth is that while I was so excited about God, Jesus, the Apostles, and doing ministry, there was nothing that could prepare me for what I was about to experience. As I look back over everything, I understand now that even at a young age, I was already being prepared for ministry just by living in an abusive home that was surrounded by alcoholism, and infidelity. Ministers who are truly sent by God, normally start out in turmoil. This why I cannot stress enough for the children of God to please be observant.

Needless to say, the excitement of ministry was short lived. During the time the disappointments of life began to manifest, I had no clue that it was all for ministry purposes and for God to get the glory out of my life. All I remember is that I went through a lot of struggles, disappointments, dark days, loneliness, and every negative emotion. Yep, I even considered the big one, SUICIDE!! I never intentionally tried to kill myself, but I did enough drinking and popping pills where I could have easily overdosed. When the troubles of life started hitting me and the pain began to penetrate to the very depths of my soul, the excitement of ministry left me really quickly. It is safe to assume that I asked, "Ministry? Ministry where? Jesus who? Ummm, the way I'm feeling, I really don't want to hear about Jesus right now." Talk about God taking care of babies and fools. I am a living witness that He does.

Lady Linda Jenise

Chapter One
Reminiscing

"And God shall wipe away all tears from their eyes; and there shall be no more death, neither sorrow, nor crying, neither shall there be any more pain: for the former things are passed away." (Revelations 21:4)

Oh my God! She is so beautiful and laying there so peacefully. Her makeup is gorgeous, hair is on point, and she is wearing my favorite leopard dress. My mother always cared about how she looked, no matter where she was going. She always said, "I want to be buried in my blue jeans, with my hair and nails done." We tried to honor her wishes, but her body was so swollen that we could not fit her into those jeans as she requested.

The casket that my father picked out for her was just beautiful. It was white with light pink and deep pink roses along with gold trim. As I looked at my mother with tears in my eyes at the confused age of fifteen, I'm sitting there thinking, "What am I going to do without my mother?" My brother, who had just been released from prison, was sitting there looking as though he was in a daze because the last time he'd seen my mother alive, he cussed her out; it was bad. He threatened to take her life. I could remember him saying, "I'll snatch you out that door, you dangled-eyed b****!" Ouch!!! Now, he has to sit here and look at her lifeless body, with no way to say, "I'm sorry Momma." He has no way to go back and take back all those hateful and hurtful things that he had said to her. Then there was my sister, who was sobbing just as much as I was.

As I looked at my mother lying in her final resting place, I hear a loud voice in the funeral home. Oh, my goodness! It is my Uncle from Detroit, Michigan. I watched him as he walked down the aisle to say goodbye to his baby sister. I had never seen so many grown men cry. All at the same time, I'm watching my father sob with uncontrollable tears streaming down his face. I couldn't help but wonder if he was crying because he is going to miss her, or if he is thinking about all the brutal beatings that he had given her. Maybe it was a mixture—I don't know— but as I watched him cry, my mind began to reminisce about when I was a child, and back to the years when I encountered many dark days, and that is to say the least.

I grew up in small town called Neelyville Missouri. There were only two stores, a church, school and train tracks. The highlight of the day was watching my dad and uncles work on their gardens.

I was maybe five years old, and laying in the bed pretending to be sleep, but all the time I'm listening to my mother scream "Book," (Book is what we called my father), "Book, stop! Why are you are doing this?" Fear began to take over me because the noise became louder and louder, and more intense. All I heard was screaming, and rumbling. It sounded like furniture being moved around. I heard my father yelling, "You b****, I'm going to show you who is the boss in this house!" It sounded like WWE going on right there in my own house. I was under the covers seeking protection the best I could as a five-year-old. I was scared to death. I was crying, confused and not understanding why the beatings were even taking place. I was young, but I knew it should not be happening.

The next morning, after my father had left for the day. I would walk into my parents' bedroom and lay on the bed with Momma.

She would pull the covers over me, and I would look at what used to be her beautiful face. It was now bruised and swollen. The vessels in her eyes were busted, she had blood stains on her lips, all along with liquor on her breath. I didn't know what that smell was at the time because I was only a child. I remember her words to me, my sister, and my brother. She said, "I don't care what your daddy does to me. He is still your father and you will respect him as such." I was thinking, Okay, but that statement did not sit so well with my brother and my sister. Well, they were older, and they understood what was really going on. My father's actions led to a lot of rebellion and disrespect from my brother. As for my sister, well, she just didn't like him. Now me on the other hand, I was a daddy's girl to my heart, and no matter what … my daddy could not do any wrong in my eyes.

Looking back, I can remember the numbness that was in my mother's eyes. As I looked into her soul, I could see nothing but hurt, emptiness, and confusion. It's like her eyes were saying, "What did I do to deserve this? What have I done?" They say the eyes are the window to the soul, so when I looked into her eyes, I saw brokenness. I saw darkness. I saw confusion. I saw a pitiful woman trying to understand. I saw a woman whose life was gone. Her eyes told me, that there was no hope; none at all.

Many times, she would be bleeding and could not move because of the pain that was inflicted upon her from the beatings. Being the baby of the family, I would just lay on her back, in tears, and we would both just cry. I used to tell her, "It's going to be all right, Momma." I would go and get her a towel and help clean her up. All she would reiterate to me was, "No matter what your daddy does to me, he is still your daddy, and you kids will respect him as such."

I remember one time my father came into the bedroom and woke us up from our sleep. He made us come into the living room, and when we got in there, he had my mother's face all busted up, and he had a gun to her head. She had blood mixed with tears running down her face. I began to scream, "Daddy, nooo!" My mom looked up at me. She only had one good eye, because the other eye he had shut from the beatings. "Book, why are you doing this to the kids?" she asked. "If you going to kill me, please don't do it in front of my children."

My sister being older remembers a lot more than I do. She told me about an incident where my father had beat my mother terribly, and then loaded all of us up in the car, took us down a back road, and put my mother out of the car. He told her, "I hope you lay here and die!" and he left her. Yep, he left her on the side of the road for her to die. After my sister told me that story, I never asked her anything else about what she remembered. I can bet that my brother remembered way more than we did because he was the oldest of us all. This explains why he didn't care for my father. Also, I believe that this was why he was so rebellious towards my father, and this eventually turned him to the alcohol bottle, just like my mother did. You talk about generational curses at its finest.

I can remember the day after the beatings, we would go to school, smiling, laughing, and pretending as if everything was okay, and the truth is, it wasn't. My home life was horrible. At this point in my life, I was just trying to keep things as normal as possible. As a kid, I remember so many nights like those, to the point that beatings became a normal thing in my home. Growing up in a home where there is abuse is not safe for children, physically, emotionally, or mentally. That type of behavior has a mental effect on children.

So what happens to the children who suffer from abuse in the homes? We grow up and that hurt matures with us. The older we get, the more that hurt manifests itself in our everyday lives mainly in our behavior. As a woman who went through this, I found myself staying in relationships that I knew meant me no good. Over time, I developed self-esteem issues, which lead to unacceptable behaviors. If we don't allow God to come in and heal our hearts completely, the pain shapes the person we become. But, I've got some good news: Jesus said, "I will keep those in perfect peace whose minds stay on me."

To a young convert or one who is a babe in Christ this can be a battle. Yes, you must fight for your sanity. You have to fight to get rid of those hurtful images that are constantly playing around in your head and tormenting your thinking. Anyone that has been through abuse, whether directly or indirectly, must understand that growing up in this type of environment can and will affect the way a child turns out as an adult. This can be negative or positive. One thing I can say is, I am so glad that Jesus was introduced to me at a young age, which gave me some type of spiritual balance. Going to church and learning about Jesus and His ways, helped me balance the abuse that I was witnessing just about every night. I know that everyone does not have that privilege, so I pray for them right now.

Prayer for Abuse in the Home

Father, I come to you as humbly as I know how. I come to You on behalf of my sisters and brothers who have gone through and those who are going through, and those who have witnessed abuse in their homes. Whether the abuse was between parents, their sisters and brothers, or whether it was directly done to them. Father, I ask that You cover them with Your Son's precious blood. I ask that You come and heal their hearts and their minds. I bind emotional trauma. I bind self-worthlessness. I bind hatred, and I bind any dark emotion that could branch off from abuse. God, I ask that You fill them with Your love, with Your peace, and with Your joy. I ask these and all blessings, in thy Son Jesus' name, Amen!

Chapter Two
She was still my Mother

"Let us walk honestly, as in the day; not in rioting and drunkenness, not in chambering and wantonness, not in strife and envying." (Romans 13:13).

Oh my God! I did NOT want to go home because I knew what awaited me. I could feel the disgust rising in my spirit as I walked on the train tracks to my house. I knew that my mother was drunk, and I did not want to hear her slurred words. I did not want to smell her liquored breath that was covered up with a nasty smelling perfume. I did not want to see her hanging off her bed because she could barely walk. Jesus, I need your help! Oh, and not to mention, who knows what man or men are going to be at the house when I get there?

"Linda, is that you?" I could hear my mother yelling.

I really did not want to answer her, but with a soft reply I answered, "Yes, Ma'am, it's me."

"Come here," she said. I went into her bedroom where the odor of alcohol lingered through the air. "Do you have a basketball game tonight?"

I so wanted to lie and say, "Nope," but I knew the consequences for lying was a beating, whether she was drunk or sober. "Yes, Ma'am," I replied.

"Ok," she said, "Let me get dressed and I will take you because I am going."

Lord knows I didn't want her to go to my game. All my friends would be there, and their sober parents would be there. Oh, my goodness. I knew that I was getting ready to be completely embarrassed. I thought, Jesus, can you please allow her to pass out or something? Guess what? She got up, put her wig on, and left for my ball game. Yay, me!

I asked her to drop me off at the side door so that I could go straight to the locker room, but the truth is, I didn't want anyone to see me get out of the car with her. I was just that embarrassed, (although I feel bad now), I didn't really understand at that time. All I knew was that I was at a ballgame where all my friends were, with my drunk mother.

It was game time. I was out on the court warming up, shooting around, and trying to avoid looking her way. I was trying to stay focused on the game at hand. All of a sudden, I saw my mother get up, and she fell right there on the gym floor. That time I didn't feel any embarrassment. My heart actually felt sorry for her. I felt sorry for my mother. I dropped the ball and ran over there to get her up from off the floor. I remember looking into her eyes, and there was a blank stare. I now know that those were hurt, and lost eyes that I looked into that night. Those eyes told me the story of a beaten and abused woman who turned to alcohol to ease her pain. My mother used alcohol to try and escape the cares of this world.

After I helped her to stand, my auntie came and took my mother home. The hurt that my mother endured was caused by the man she vowed to love. On their wedding day, I could imagine her saying, "I do vow to love you for the rest of my life," but she didn't know that loving him would cost her so much pain, and on several occasions, almost her life.

As a kid coming up, it was hard for me to recognize the drunken behavior, because I was only a child. However, the older I got, the more aware of the behavior I became. Often, I was in denial, because not only was I dealing with the beatings in my home but learning to deal with a drunk in the house. So much for a normal life.

I helped my mother up from off the floor numerous times. Sometimes there was a certain look that she had; I just knew that she was not there mentally. Her drunken behavior had gotten so bad that I did not want to have friends over. I didn't want to be there myself, but I felt sorry for her, after all, she was my mother. I literally had to feed and take care of myself because she spent most of her life passed out in her room. That is one trait that I did get from her—being isolated in my bedroom.

She would be so drunk that she would urinate on herself, and I had to sometimes clean her. It was just a horrible experience at that time, but now I know that my father's abuse is what brought about the alcoholism. Because she died when I was a young girl, I never got to question her about her childhood. I believe that if my mother were alive today, she would tell me that she was the victim of rape and or molestation.

The interesting thing was that my mother attended church all the time. She made sure that I stayed in the church. I understand now, that no matter what she did, she was charged by the Holy Spirit to make sure that I was in church so that I could grow spiritually. Although she was a drunk, that drunk kept me in church, which was the best thing that could have ever happened to me. I loved going to church. It was where I had peace, freedom, and I could be a kid. I absolutely loved it!!!

I know it doesn't sound like a great childhood, however, I can say that I was fortunate because I had the Holy Spirit working in this dark season of my life. I can now look back over the course of my life and see how the Holy Spirit was in control the entire time. I can see how He protected me physically, and how He protected my sanity in these "dry places." The Holy Spirit kept my heart soft, and He kept the love in my heart for my mother and my father. Regardless of what they did, how they acted, or what they said. I know because of the Holy Spirit that was operating in my life that I could never hate them. Yes, much of my childhood I was embarrassed, but hate…NEVER!!!

The demon of alcoholism is real, and it is very much alive. This is why we as children of God, must be careful when we are trying to judge someone. We look at a person's outer actions to dictate who they are, or we make assumptions based on how they act. For example, when we see a person that is addicted to alcohol or drugs, we automatically make it up in our minds that he or she is just a no-good junkie. When the truth of the matter is that we don't know the hurt, the pain, or trauma that someone is carrying around. They could have been raped or lost a loved one, and it pushed them to use other coping mechanisms, such as drugs or alcohol. Church folks, hear me and hear me well. Keep your mouth off other people! I don't care if they are a sinner or saint. We don't know the hurt that they are harboring around in their heart. So many self-righteous people who may have not had to face what some of the addicts have had to face, then to judge – they just need to get somewhere and sit down.

I can hear the church folks now. "Well, I've been hurt, and I didn't do that. I didn't turn to the alcohol bottle. I turned to Jesus." You should be thankful that God kept you from using the bottle and kept you from using other drugs. I can guarantee you one thing, that if you have suffered severe hurt in your life, then you are carrying some of the residues. You may say, "No I don't." I will say, "Yes you do." It's just the residue that has grown and matured with you. When residue attaches itself to you, it becomes a part of who you are. Why do you think there are so many *mean* people in churches? These people attend church faithfully, but they are something else. Most of church folks that I have met are mean, nasty, and spiritually ugly. Why do you think that is so? It's because they need to be delivered from past pain, and they don't even realize it. They have become one with their nastiness, and it is now comfortable to them, so they don't recognize that it is even there. They don't even realize when they are mean or nasty to someone because it had become their norm. Ask me how I know? Yep, you guessed it. That used to be me. Therefore, it is so important that we ask God to reveal our hearts to ourselves on a daily basis. We must ask God to cleanse us every day, or we will end up just like the church folk that I just described - bitter and mean!

In ministry, I can see now how the past pain that my mother endured, God has used it for me to be able to reach those with a same or similar pain. The Holy Spirit carried me through it so that I can use it for ministry in this season. The Holy Spirit taught me through the pain of life that everyone doesn't weather the storm the same. The truth is, my mother died when I was fifteen years old, and I still don't know what she suffered as a child growing up. Did her upbringing as a child play a part in how she handled the storms of her life? I am sure it did. The truth is, you, me, and fifteen other people, can go through the same storm and all seventeen of us will come out with different results. Some will be spiritually stronger. Some will be suicidal, and some will be addicts to the drug of their choice. It all depends on what kind and how much spiritual DNA is running through our blood. For example, I cannot expect a new convert or a babe in Christ to handle the storm as I would. I don't know if they have been taught Jesus, how much Jesus they were taught, or if they were even taught the real Jesus. I was taught how to incorporate the Word in my daily life, but everybody did not have the luxury of having an alcoholic mother, an abusive father, all while being taught the goodness of Jesus in their lives. I was taught by the Spirit of the Holy Ghost to seek after God at an early age, and that all came from my alcoholic mother seeing to it, that I made it to church every Sunday. Thank you, Marie Conley. You saved my life!

Prayer for Families Dealing with Alcoholism

Dear most gracious, and caring Father. Sometimes we don't understand why You lead us to the valleys of life, but we know that all things work together for the good for those that love you and who are called according to Your purpose. Father, I pray for any family that is dealing with the demonic spirit of alcoholism. I bind that spirit right now in the righteous name of Jesus. I take authority over the enemy right now through the anointing of the Holy Ghost. In the name of Jesus, I curse the demon of alcoholism at the root and I cast you back to the pits of hell. I curse the generational curse of alcoholism, seven generations forward and seven generations backward. I declare and decree that the Blood is purified through the Blood of the Lamb. I plead the Blood over the families right now. I command that spirit to lose that loved one right now in the name of Jesus. I stand in the gap for anyone that has experienced this pain. I petition the throne of grace on their behalf. I bind the chains of heaviness that come from the troubles and cares of this world. Father God, heal them, deliver them, restore them, and set them free in Jesus. I come against every dark force that is trying to attach itself to them to prevent them from experiencing Your love, Your joy, and most definitely Your peace. Satan, I strip you of your devices, you have no legal rights to God's Children. In Jesus' name, Amen!

Battle Behind the Sword

Lady Linda Jenise

Chapter Three
My House was not a Home

Marriage is honorable among all, and the bed undefiled: but whoremongers and adulterers God will judge" (Hebrews 13:4).

My father was a truck driver who was on the road about two weeks at a time. This type of set up is not good for any marriage. This type of set up is a recipe for disaster and a for sure divorce. When I would come home from a school event, I could expect one, two, or three things that were going to happen at my house when daddy was on the road. One, momma was going to be drunk; two, she was going to be holy and playing gospel music; or three, there was going to be one or more men, at my house – none of whom was my father. Lord, who will be at my house when I get there tonight? I often wondered.

My mother was sleeping with numerous men. Some of them were "hit men." I remember how they used to sit up and talk about how they killed someone, and where they dumped the body. I can understand now why they were doing lines of cocaine. If I were a "hit-man," I would need some type of narcotic as well. I remember when my sister's boyfriend did her wrong, and my mother asked my sister if she wanted to have him *killed*. My sister knew that my mother was serious, so she, my sister responded, "Nooooo, I'm good on that!"

My mother would take me to hotels with her. This was the most horrible experience that a child could ever go through. I watched some of these men do cocaine through "snorting." It was just a terrible sight. Sometimes there would be several of them, and then they would all pass out from drinking and doing drugs. I was scared to go to sleep, but my mother kept me real close to her when there was more than one man around. One thing I can say is that she protected me physically, but I don't think she gave it any thought when it came to how this exposure would affect me mentally.

Momma laid on the bed and laid me on the bed with them. I was on one side, the gentleman was on the other side, and she was in the middle. I think the idea was that I was supposed to be sleeping, but all the while I was listening to the moans, groans and the movements under the sheets. To this day I can still hear and feel the uncomfortableness, just like it was yesterday. I was only a child, but I knew in the pits of my stomach that this was not right. Even though I was with my mother, I was a scared little girl who wanted the protection of her father. I think this was the creepiest feeling that I have ever felt, but the truth is told, the more it happened, the more I got used to it. I got used to the trips to the hotel, laying in a bed with my mother and man who was not my daddy.

While my dad was on the road, there were many men in and out of our house. I watched my mother take men back to her bedroom. One day I was sitting there watching TV, and my mother had one of her male friends back in the bedroom. I sat there, and I heard a loud truck. The problem was, we lived by a train track, so we heard those sounds all the time. There was something different about this sound, though, because then I heard a loud "Shh!". It sounded like opening a soda can, and the fizz sound that comes out, except the sound was incredibly loud, and stronger. I got up, ran to the window, and I saw "the snake," which was my dad's eighteen-wheeler. He got that name because he parked his truck just like a snake in front of the house.

You would think that I would have run to the back to let my mother know, but nope. I was so excited to see my father; I ran to the door to let him in. As a child, I wasn't too concerned about the fact that another man was in his room. I was just happy to see him. He gave me my Vienna sausages and my honey buns, as usual, and he proceeded to go the back of the house. Oh boy, and there it went.

Luckily, they weren't doing anything in the bedroom, but my dad was so mad, he picked the guy up with one hand, drug him to the front room, and threw him out of the house. My dad then beat my mother senseless. I don't think it mattered at that time, because she was so drunk, and I believe she had become immune to the beatings.

I used to get sick when I came home from school and saw those cars, and vans, at our house. Some of the men would ask, "Marie, how is old is your daughter?" She would come unglued and would pull her pistol out on them and tell them I dare you to even think about anything like that about my baby. It was just an awful place for a young lady to be. Momma was from Detroit – she was very feisty and feared no one. When it came to protecting her children, she would do so at all cost. Trust and believe, she always kept her pistol within arm's reach.

Parents should not ever put their children in this type of environment, especially little girls. By no means am I making excuses for my mother, but I know now that she was a wounded woman looking for love. When a woman's heart has been bruised and scorned, she will seek out love through her bruised and scorned eyes. Having those kinds of eyes will cause you to see deceit camouflaged in love. I can't blame her for anything that she put me through because she didn't know any better. That is why it is imperative for women to allow God to heal their brokenness before they go searching for love. If they do not allow God to heal them, they will attract the same kind of man, over and over and over again.

I am not saying that my mother's actions were justified, but they are explainable. Also, guess who did the same thing when they got older? You guessed it, me! When this behavior was prevalent in my life, I did not realize that this was a generational curse that needed to be broken. I was a broken woman; I was also empty due to the experiences of my childhood, and the loss of my mother. I was trying to find something to fill in my void. I was trying to find something that made me feel whole and complete. So I did what I knew how to do, which was to seek the love of men.

The truth of the matter is God is the only man that could fill that deep and empty void. When we are down and feel like there is a lack in our lives, we must immediately seek God for His intimacy, because a man can't make us feel complete, whole and satisfied. It is in that deepest, darkest, and loneliest hour that God wants to become one with us and wants to restore us. It is in that place that He wants to heal us, love us, rock us, cradle us, and tell us how special and beautiful we are to Him.

For Him to be that man to us, we must seek Him. Without seeking Christ, we will stay in a broken and bruised place. If we are not healed by the love of Christ, then we will go into a relationship and we will love our significant other with a broken and bruised heart. That relationship will only be temporary. It takes a complete and whole love to keep a relationship together, and we know that kind of love can only come through Jesus Christ.

Prayer for the Little Girls or Boys Who are in an Abusive Environment

Dear most gracious God, I come on behalf of my sisters and my brothers, who are in an environment where they don't feel safe, or they don't understand what is going on. Father, I ask that You allow Your angels to shield and protect them from all hurt, harm, and danger. I ask that You let Your angels stand charge and encamp around them and protect them. I ask that You hold them right in the cradle of Your arms. Rock them in the midnight hour.

Father God make them know that it may not seem like it, but You are right there to make sure no harm comes to them. You said in your Word that You would never leave us, nor forsake us. I ask that You protect their mind, their sanity, their emotions, and their will. Father, I ask that You allow them to walk through this fire and come out as pure gold—no residue left on them—and if there is, let it be used for ministry purposes.

Even those who have been through this dark situation and seem lost. Father make them know that You anointed them to go through the fire, and now they must go and help pull their sister and their brother out of the fire. Lord help them find peace in the storm. Father, I come against the enemy tactics and every negative thing that Satan is trying to throw at them mentally. I come against every plot, plan, and scheme that Satan is trying to use as a hindrance to stop them from walking in their divine purpose. Satan, the Lord rebukes you in Jesus' name. Satan, I bind you up in the name of Jesus, and I cast you back to the pits of hell from where you came. "Let this mind be in my bother and my sister that was also in Christ Jesus." Father, I thank You for all that You have done, and all that You are going to do. I give You all of the honor, the glory, and the praise. In Jesus name, Amen!

Battle Behind the Sword

Chapter Four
The Day Momma Left Me

"Jesus said unto her, I am the resurrection, and the life: he that believeth in me, though he were dead, yet shall he live: And whosoever liveth and believeth in me shall never die. Believest thou this?'" (John 11:25-26).

This day was just as normal as any other day. My mother had stopped drinking and had been sober for a long time at this point. She woke up really sick, and she was throwing up green fluids. I was taking care of her while she just laid in her bedroom, continually throwing up. I asked her on several occasions, "Momma, do you need to go to the hospital?" "No!" she replied. I went on about my day. I was sitting watching TV when she came in the living room, bent over and holding her stomach. You could tell that she was in a lot of pain because she could not even stand up straight. She could barely walk, and in her little, weak voice, she said, "I need to go to the hospital." I was only fifteen years old and did not have a driver's license, but I could drive. Of course, when you grow up in the country, you learn to drive starting at about ten years old. I was introduced to driving by driving a tractor with my father, so by the age of fifteen, I could drive anything. My mother knew that I could drive too, so she did not hesitate about giving me the car keys. In my mind, I thought that we would go to the hospital, they would give her a little medicine, and then we would be right back home.

I took her to the hospital and they checked her in. I will never forget it: she had on a green jogging suit, and she was lying on the hospital bed, still throwing up green stuff. The nurses went and got her a little white tray for her to puke in. She was lying on her back, on that gurney in agony, still holding her stomach. Her eyes were red and watery. Anyone could look at her and tell she was not doing well. After the doctor came in, he said to her, "We are going to keep you, so that we can find out why you are throwing up." Again, they did not seem concerned or anything. Momma sent me home and told me to go and get her some clothes, deodorant, soap, and some other personal things.

I did as I was told. I went and got the things that Momma

requested, dropped them off at the hospital and left. In my fifteen-year-old mind, I thought that I had a car and the house all to myself. Yep, it's party time! I did just that, but I made sure to be at that hospital every day to check on her. I remember the night before she died, I went to see her. She told me, "I get out in the morning, so be here at 8:00 a.m." I said, "Yes ma'am," and went to my friend's house to celebrate my last party.

Later that same night, my cousin came in looking tore up. She could barely walk, and she could hardly talk. I had to ask her about ten questions because all she could do was nod her head, but she could not force any words out. Then, I finally asked the question that I dreaded. "Is it Momma?" She nodded "Yes," with tears running down her face. Was bent over and could barely breathe. "Is she ok?" I asked. She tried to shake her head "No." I said, "Dead?" Again, she could barely shake her head, but it wasn't a nod for "No" this time. She looked at me and nodded her head "Yes."

OH, MY GOD!! I believe that I had never heard such devastating words in my life, nor had I ever felt such pain in my life. It was a feeling that is unexplainable. I honestly believe that I was in shock, and for the first time in my life, I was speechless. At that time, all I knew was that I had to get to the hospital. My cousins drove me, but I don't believe it really hit me until I got there. I remember going up to the hospital and having a fit. I yelled and cried so hard that I was literally making myself sick. The nurses said to me, "Linda, before we bring her out, we need to calm you down." The nurse asked if it was okay that they give me a shot to calm me down. I agreed to the shot. However, the shot did absolutely nothing for me. They wheeled me down to the morgue, and they pulled my mother out, and she was stiff as a board. I remember touching her, and she was ice cold. I still remember how beautiful she was lying there. My mother was a very attractive woman with an hourglass figure. Everything seemed like a dream to me, so it wasn't registering with me quite yet. I went home and got some rest. I woke up, hoping that everything was a huge nightmare. My father was on the road. I was at the house by myself, and I remember that I wanted to take my mother's pistol and take my own life. I remember right when I was considering suicide, my mother's cousin came over with my six-month-old nephew, and the joy he brought me at that time was the only thing that stopped me from killing myself. I just loved on him and cried, and loved on him some more, and kept crying. I thought, "God, what am I going to do? I am fifteen years old, and my mother is dead."

I don't remember anything else after that except the funeral. I always remembered my mother saying, "I don't want no funeral. I don't want anybody whooping and hollering over me and, bury me in my jeans. Ha!" She got some of what she requested. She got a wake. It was sort of like a funeral, just minus the singing and preaching. We buried her in a dress suit. Honestly, we did try to have her buried in her jeans, but as I mentioned earlier, she was too swollen, so she could not fit into them.

That was when I really questioned the validity of God's existence. What about this gracious and merciful God that I was taught? How could a God that is so wonderful take away a mother from her fifteen-year-old child? Why would this God do such a terrible thing? At that point, I was so angry with God for taking my mother, that I figured I would get back at Him. I figured what better way to get back at God than to do that which He is dead against - sin. I decided to do just what I had been taught which is lay on my back for whoever. Even though I knew that it was wrong, it is still what I had been taught.

I started sleeping with men from left to right. I turned to alcohol, popping pills, and smoking weed. Pills were my thing. I would have had to have taken some kind of drug before I slept with the men. The more drugs I did, the more men I slept with to mask and ease my pain. I tried not to allow myself to connect with them emotionally, but there were some that I did make an emotional connection. My father was a truck driver, so he was never home. I had the house to myself to do whatever I wanted to do. It was the emptiest feeling. After I was done having sex with those men, I almost hated myself. Sometimes, I would just sit and cry, and then I drunk more alcohol and popped more pills. I lived for alcohol and to get high. At that time, I had not realized that those demons that were taking over me were inherited. They were a generational curse. I was actually repeating my mother's life all over again.

Nobody could tell me nothing. After all, I didn't have to answer to anyone. In my young mind, Momma was gone, and my father was a truck driver who lived on the road, so therefore I had no one to answer to or tell me what to do. My father was gone, but he sent money every week, so I was good. I didn't have to worry about God because our relationship was done; it was a wrap. I wasn't thinking about church, God, Jesus, nor the Holy Ghost.

One day, I was out in the garden talking with my aunt. I told her about all of the wrongs that I was doing. She had that spirit that seemed like it compelled me to just started confessing on my own. She was the most righteous and sweetest woman that I had ever known. She was surely an angel of the Lord. Obviously, this behavior pattern was not unusual to her because she and my mother were close. Then out of the blue, she said to me, "You are not your mother," while she kept chopping the weeds in her garden.

I was in shock because I didn't understand the value of that comment. I thought, "I know that because I am Linda!" (smile). By now I was a little older and a little more hot-headed, so it just kind of went over my head. But for a long time, those little bitty words resonated in my spirit for a very long time. I didn't really understand what she meant but coming from her I knew that it was something that I needed to hear.

One night, my cousin and I went to Sikeston, Missouri to go to the club. On our way there, the car stopped dead in the middle of the road. We could not get the doors opened because they were closed with a rope tied around them (talk about a contraption!). It just so happened that there was an eighteen-wheeler barreling towards us. He started honking, but we could not move. I began to pray and ask God to help us, and immediately the car cranked up, and we got off the road, right in the nick of time. I got to my cousin's house, and instead of going to the club I called my aunt. She said to me, "Hun, the Bible says to never leave your first love" (meaning God). I remember looking out the window that Sunday. I watched people get in their cars, headed to church, and I remember saying, "That's where I need to be going." The next weekend I went back home and went to church.

I was working at a well-known chicken plant, and there I met a man. I was not interested at all, but everyone kept telling me he was a security blanket and that I need to snatch him up. So I kept talking to him, and we eventually got married. I can honestly tell you that I got married because I thought that God would get me if we lived together without being married. I was not in love, and I knew it, but I knew that this man would take care of me. About one year later I found out that he was nine years older than what he originally told me, and he was also still married when he started seeing me. So the whole marriage was based on a lie; no wonder it didn't work! However, I was dealing with a lot of issues of my own, except, I didn't know they were issues. Does that make sense?

I was bitter, mean, loud, spoiled, and aggressive - and everything else that was not good. The problem was, these were the same demonic spirits that my mother had, and now those demons had rested on me. The interesting thing is, I never knew those demonic spirits were there because they had become comfortable to me. I never thought for one minute that I had issues. In my mind, it was all Stan's (my husband) - all of the problems that I had were all his fault. It was nothing for me to talk down to this man, and degrade him, just because that is who I was, and I didn't see anything wrong with it. After all, he allowed it. I would talk to this man as if I was talking to a child.

Stan was dealing with his own issues in addition to continually cheating on me. It was a never-ending cycle. But now I realize that I brought those inherited demons into the marriage, which resulted in a lot of bitterness and anger towards him. The bitterness and anger had become so comfortable to me, that it was literally who I was, and I did not even know it. That is why, when a couple is getting married, it is very important that they not only counsel with a man of God to make sure their spirits are right, but both parties need healing of their emotions as well. That means any past issues that are weighing on them need to be brought to the surface so that God can come in and heal them. It is also very important that the Man of God who is doing the counseling is a true "Man of God." The reason is, he will have a spirit of discernment which will be able to discern the brokenness between the two individuals. This needs to take place first, for both parties. Just as my marriage was - two broken people that marry each other is a recipe for a future train wreck.

Leaders need to make sure that they are using spiritual discernment when counseling married and engaged couples. After about two minutes of conversation, spiritual leaders should be able to tell who is bitter, who is broken, who needs to be delivered, and or who needs to be restored. Then the spirit of God should guide everything that is needed to heal them.

In this generation, I am seeing where church leaders are pushing people into marriage, all so that it can look good on their church roster. They feel as though once they are married, then they can put them in a position in the church. Whatever the reason may be, the leaders who are doing this needs to stop. You are ruining these people's lives. Also, don't you know God is going to hold you accountable?

One day, after putting up with all of what Stan was doing to me, I decided that I was going to cheat back. I kept hearing the Lord say, "Don't do it," and I said, "But God, I'm tired of him cheating on me, so I am cheating back." Of course, I already had in mind the man with whom I wanted to have an affair. I had been faithful to my husband up until now. In my mind, his cheating gave me a license to cheat back. I was not living anywhere near the spiritual realm, to say the least. I went ahead and I cheated Stan with the man that I already wanted to sleep with, and guess what happened? I fell in love with him.

He and I began to spend more time together. We would have long conversations, and he made me laugh. This guy actually had a personality, which is something that Stan did not have. This man was very romantic and very sweet to me. Looking back, I can see how I was deceived by my own desires and I was justified in committing adultery because Stan had committed adultery. I am not looking for anyone to blame, not even the enemy. The devil had nothing to do with this affair; this was all Linda's doing. The fact that this man was everything that I had wanted made it easier for me to keep falling deeper and deeper in love with him. In other words, adultery or sinning felt wonderful to my flesh, and no, I did not want to come out of it.

The problem with living in sin is when you belong to God, He will not allow you to find any peace in the sin. One Sunday I was in church and it was hot in the sanctuary. To me it seemed like the roof of the church was caving in on me. Trust me when I say, I never got any peace or rest when I stepped outside the will of God. The people at the church would ask me to do testimony service or devotion and I answered, "Nope!" I knew better. They would *not* have to sit me down. When I know that I am living a life of sin, I will sit my own self down. I told my pastor and my cousins what I was doing. They tried to counsel me, but I was doing what Linda wanted to do......period!

One Sunday on my way back from church, I heard the spirit of the Lord say, "Linda, do you love your sin more than you love me?" First, I said, "Uh?" Then I heard it again, "Linda, do you love your sin more than you love me?" I became so remorseful, then before I knew it, I began to cry uncontrollably. My spirit was heavy because the reality was setting in, and the reality was that I had sinned against God. While driving and crying, I answered, "No, Lord. I don't love my sin more than I love you." The Lord said, "Well, come out of it." "But Lord, he cheated on me," I responded. This is where I learned that God doesn't judge us based on how someone else treated us, but he judges us based on how we treat them. I finally submitted and said, "Okay, God. I can't do this on my own. You are going to have to help me."

This is where I learned to work the Word of God into my life and my situation. The first thing that I did was quit answering the phone when the other man called. I eventually ended up changing my phone number. Let me help somebody; when it comes to salvation, we must do whatever it takes. If it means cutting people's communication methods off or cutting the people themselves off, then do what you got to do. See I was in a fight for spirituality, so I was down to do whatever it took. I also quit going to the places where he would hang out. I was in a spiritual critical care unit. I stayed home and read my Bible. Many times, I read my Bible with tears in my eyes because I was in love with another man and I was missing him like crazy. But, I had it in my spirit that I loved God more than I loved my sin, so whatever it took I was willing to go through it. I had to stay in spiritual isolation until God came in and healed me. Which means God came in and removed all desires that I had for the other man. I knew when I had been delivered because I would see the man at a ball game or similar event and felt no desire to be with him.

Still to this day, I don't feel any desire for him. I eventually told my husband what I had done, and asked for his forgiveness although, he never apologized to me for the things that he did. Never receiving an apology was ok with me because this was about Linda's salvation.

The truth of the matter is, I never cheated to get back at Stan. I cheated because I was not in love, and I just wanted something different. I just used the fact that he was cheating on me as an excuse to do something that I already wanted to do. I honestly had no business getting married with all the stuff that I had been through and was never healed and delivered. There is no way that I believe a person can say that he or she belongs to God and are comfortable with a sinful lifestyle.

Prayer for Having Anger against God because of the death of a Loved One.

Dear most gracious Father. I petition the throne of Grace on behalf of my sisters and my brothers, who feel as though you have let them down. For those who have developed anger and animosity in their hearts against You and have given up and lost all hope. I pray for restoration right now, in the name of Jesus. Allow them to know that sometimes you will allow things to happen to us, to help us, even if it hurts us. Help them to know that there is an appointed time for man to live, and there is an appointed time for man to die. I pray that you make them know that even in our darkest hour, you are still with us. Let my sisters and my brothers know there are a lot of things that happen to us in life that we don't understand, but it is in that hour that we must hold on to Your hand and stand on your word. Father God make them know that the pain that you have allowed is designed to push us closer to you. I curse anger at the root in Jesus' name. Father, I pray that you send your ministering angels to my sister and my brother, who are hurting, and who are confused. Allow the angels to minister to their grieving souls. Father, I pray for a release like no other. I pray for restoration like never before. I pray for a change of heart like never before. I pray for their heart to be un-hardened in Jesus' name. Father, no matter what disappointments we may face on this journey, make my brothers and sisters to know that your love, mercy, and grace are the only things that are strong enough to carry us through. In Jesus' name, AMEN!

Chapter Five
Nobody's Little Girl

"The righteous perisheth and no man layeth it to heart: and merciful men are taken away, none considering that the righteous is taken away from the evil to come. He shall enter into peace: they shall rest in their beds, each one walking in His uprightness." (Isaiah 57: 1-2).

After my mother's death, my father made a spiritual change. The truth is my mother and father had gotten divorced in previous years, but yet they stayed together. They actually got along much better after the divorce (how does that make sense?) After Momma died, Daddy became such a peaceful man, to the point where he could not stand confusion or drama of any kind. He wouldn't even be around confusion. He became the peace-maker of the family as well as the family counselor. The family would go and talk to him whenever they were having issues. His whole character changed. Not only did he become a peace-maker, but he also became an unintentional comedian. He would say some of the funniest things. He had a brother that he was very close too; they were one in the same. They argued over the funniest things. They were a delight to be around. If we were having a dreadful day, just going and being in the presence of these two gentlemen, we would forget about our troubles because of the laughter that we would experience.

This man that I call Daddy now is no-where near the same man that I saw beating my mother every night. This is what happens when God enters a person's life. He comes in and gives a new life, a new walk, and a new talk. What is very interesting is that I had no bitterness, or resentment towards my father. When we are walking with God, and seeking His face, there is no way that we can remain the same. There was no way that I can seek the face of God, and still, hold resentment in my heart for my father. Seeking the face of God means searching His characteristics, His ways and His thoughts. For there to be a change in our lives, we must seek the mind of Christ. There is no way that God can do a new thing in our lives if we continue to hold onto the past.

So many times, we hold on to what was done to us, or how someone betrayed or treated us. Yes, I understand that there are some situations that cut deeper than others. For instance, I may have been betrayed by a lie in the past, but that is nothing compared to someone who has been raped or molested by an uncle, brother, or by someone they loved and trusted. Rape and molestation are wounds that run long, deep, and dark. It will literally take an act of God for deliverance in those areas. However, we must get it in our minds that we are letting go of the pain at all cost. What do I mean by "all cost?" That means we have to dig deep in the dark places of our souls and forgive those that hurt us. We must dig deep and go to the parts of our souls where all of the hurt, pain, betrayal, rape, molestation or whatever it is, is hidden. Where ever we have buried our dark truths, that is the place that we must go, resurrect it and lay it all at the feet of God. We must acknowledge to God in details the pain that we feel, the pain that we witnessed. I think many times we are scared to tell God how we feel. Newsflash! He knows anyway. He wants us to trust Him enough to share it with Him. When we share our pain with Him, this lets Him know that we are looking to Him to heal us.

Another truth is, we may have to go to someone and talk about the betrayals just to liberate ourselves. Even if it means that we must accept an apology that was never offered, then so be it. We have got to come out of agreement with the pain. We may have to do additional spiritual warfare, such as fast and pray for God to remove any anger and hatred. Listen, my friend, we are in a fight for our peace as well as our sanity, so at all cost be victorious!

Why must we let the hurt and betrayal go? Because sometimes we wear the residue of the pain on our sleeves, and it prevents us from walking into our new season, our God-ordained season. Isaiah 43: 18-19 says, "Forget the former things; do not dwell on the past. See, I am doing a new thing! Now it springs up; do you not perceive it? I am making a way in the wilderness and the streams in the wasteland."

There are some dry areas in our lives that we need the streams and the rivers to flow through. We need the rivers of the Holy Spirit to flow through our marriages, children, finances, and through our minds. But, the one thing that the scripture is very clear about is that we can't get the river to flow by holding on to the past. Tell yourself today, "I'm letting it go. I am not the same person that I used to be. I am a new creature in Christ. Old things have passed away, and behold all things have become new, in Jesus' name."

After my mother's passing, my father remarried, and she was the love of his life. I was a little jealous because at first, I could not understand why he treated this woman like a queen, but constantly beat my mother. Looking back, I can now see that was just the enemy trying to get into my head. One of the enemy's number one tool is to get into our thoughts and cause separation and division. If he can cause division in our minds, then he knows that division in the flesh is within arm's reach. I am so glad that the enemy did not win, and we remained a family. I can honestly say that I was so happy that my father finally, finally experienced true love and happiness. I was also glad that he was able to give and receive true love. His second wife adored him. She was just as funny as he was, so they were one in the same.

Unfortunately, after about three years of marriage, my father lost his second wife to cancer. He seemed to be holding up pretty well. My sister and I stayed with him as much as we could, keeping him occupied by making him laugh, or making him just be his funny self or make him fuss. My favorite thing to get a reaction from him was to park on his grass. I knew once I pulled up and he saw my car on his grass, he would be coming out of the house fussing; it never failed. My sister and I made it a point to go down to his house after work, every day just to get him out of the house. His brother also made sure that he was there to help him get through it as well.

About seven years later, my father had a stroke and was rushed to the hospital. A blood vessel in his head erupted which put him in a coma. He was not responding to the doctors, but when he heard me and my sister's voice, he started bucking and jumping. He could not say anything, but he let us know that he heard us. The doctors wanted the family to decide on whether to pull the plug on him or go through with brain surgery. The odds were not in our favor. The doctors gave us a rundown on what could possibly happen if he underwent surgery. He could be a vegetable, and possibly die. However, not having the surgery our only course of action then was to make him as comfortable as possible until he went home to be with the Lord. Oh, it was bad. We had to make a conscious decision from a place of desperation, being scared and uncertainty. What do we do God? Do we want him in a vegetative state, or do we want him dead? Or do we just trust you and not the doctors?

We decided to have the brain surgery and trust God. After the surgery, he was healing so much that the doctors could not believe what their eyes were witnessing. It was nothing more than a miracle. The doctors shared with us that there is a line in the middle of our head, and when my dad had his stroke, the whole line shifted to the left, but after the surgery, his line immediately lined back up perfectly. They asked if we would allow them to put his x-rays out so that people could see the miracle!

My dad was in a coma for two months after the surgery. He woke up on July 1st, 2004, on my twin cousins' birthday. When he woke up, his memory picked right back up where it had left off. He didn't remember the stroke at all. In his mind, there was no lapse, so we went with it. He was healing well. He was doing so well that the doctors quit seeking approvals and answers from my sister and me, instead started talking directly to my dad. Talk about a miracle!

"Book, if something was to happen to you, do you want to be resuscitated?" The doctors asked him.

"Nope!" Dad answered before I could get a word out.

"Yes, he does." I then responded.

"No, I don't!" He insisted as he looked at me.

"He is out of his mind!" I looked at the doctor waiting for his agreement.

"Okay, let's see," The doctor answered in a matter of fact voice. He then proceeded to ask Daddy questions like, "Where were you born? How old are you? How many children do you have?"

"Out of all of the times you want to be sane, you pick now!" I whispered to myself as this man answered every question correctly! I gave God glory, but I was ready to ring Daddy's neck. I'm not going to lie, I am a Daddy's girl to my heart, and I was trying desperately to hold onto my father for dear life.

"He is pretty competent." The doctor looked at me and said, He notated my dad's chart as, NO RESUSCITATION!!

For rehabilitation purposes, my sister and I agreed to put my dad in a nursing home. He was doing really well, but despite his healing, the nursing home did not take care of him as they stated they would. They did not rehabilitate him at all. They allowed him to get a bedsore and then failed to tell us about it. We didn't know anything about bedsore for a long time. I remember when my sister went to see him, she called me from the hospital. She was so upset that she could barely talk. I asked her to calm down then I asked her what was wrong. She was yelling about how she was sitting there and kept smelling something foul. She said, "I kept checking Daddy to see if he had used the bathroom on himself, but that wasn't it. I sat there, and I sat there, but I kept smelling this odor that smelled like something was rotting. The nurse finally came in to check on him, and I told her what I kept smelling. The nurse checked him, and when she unwrapped that tape that was on his back and the stench that came from his back! It was so strong and bad that I almost fainted! His flesh was literally rotting!"

I became so sick and disgusted with the nursing home, with God, everything and everyone. "Yep, here I go again!" I thought. God, I have served You, and I have worked for You, and I have trusted You, and this is what You allow to happen? Good God all mighty, how much more will You allow me to go through? Can I tell you one thing though? That was a *terrible, terrible* question to ask God.

When we found out about the bedsore, guess what? It was too late - the infection had poisoned his entire bloodstream, - the sore was so big and deep that I could put my fist through it. We took him home and took care of him there. My dad was a true soldier of the Lord. Once the spiritual conversion took place in his life, he was a man of peace. I loved that about him. One of the things that I learned from him is what it meant to fight the good fight of faith.

When we were coming down to the end of his journey, I would always get him up and out of the bed as if nothing was wrong. I still made him do things on his own because I still wanted him to have his manhood. He was still my father, my head, and the leader of the house, regardless of what shape he was in physically. I remember a conversation we had one day as he was sitting in his recliner chair. "Daddy, how is your faith?" I asked.

"My faith is fine, what about yours?" He chuckled.

"I am trusting God all the way," I answered.

"Me too," He replied. Then he said, "I know the Almighty is

coming for me; I'm just waiting."

I knew exactly what he was talking about, but I did not want to entertain that thought. I said to myself, "You ain't going nowhere," but the reality of it was that he already knew that he was getting ready to leave me, and he seemed as though he was perfectly fine with it.

Talk about a warrior, OMG! He was looking death right in the face and gave God praise all the way through it. We were singing those old-time gospel songs together. I could be sitting in the hospital room, and I would just start singing,

I can see so much,
See so much

and after a while daddy would say,

What the Lord…

I said,
Lord, my God has done me for me.

One day we were singing and had an audience and didn't even realize it. One lady just cried as he and I were singing. Those and how he was a warrior, were some memories that I carried with me. Sometimes his strength gets me through a lot of my own pain.

Thankfully, God spared him long enough so that I could prepare myself. I still say that God wanted to take him on May 12, 2004, when he had the stroke, but I wasn't ready. God allowed him to be weaned from me in a sense. Some may think I am crazy, but if they understood the spiritual realm, it does not seem crazy. No matter how many times we brought daddy home, he could not get comfortable and stay. He would stay two to three days, and something would happen, and he would have to go to the hospital. That is how God weaned him from me. He would not allow us to get comfortable with him being at home because he was going to be leaving us shortly.

On Feb 6, 2005, I was at church where I made the comment that I was okay if Daddy stayed here on earth, or if God called him home. Either way, I would still be okay. In a spiritual sense, I released my father to the spiritual realm. Because right after church, at about two p.m. that Sunday, my father passed away. We had his funeral on Feb 9, 2005. It was a home going celebration. There was singing, shouting, dancing, and rejoicing at his funeral. It was a sad time. Nevertheless, we had church because he had given his life to the Lord and he lived a peaceful life. As a family, we had every reason to give God glory. Yes, even at a funeral, God is still worthy of the praise.

Prayer for Those Dealing With a Sick Loved One

Father, I come to you in the name of Jesus, asking you to strengthen those who are taking care of a sick loved one. I ask that you strengthen them spiritually, emotionally and physically. God, it's not easy seeing our loved one go through so much pain, and there is nothing that we can do to help them. God, we even stand in the gap for our loved ones, asking that you would come in and sup with them. God, lighten the load. In Jesus' name, we ask that you carry the burden. God, I ask that you come in and supply all of the families' needs. Not only is it hard to take care of a loved one who is sick. It's even harder when you don't have the funds to get up and down the road to get medications that they need, or to get them to their doctors' appointments, or to get the specific supplies that they need. God, I ask that you send an abundance to the families in Jesus' name. Father, I ask that you give them the grace to keep looking to the hills from which cometh their help and make them know that all of their help comes from You. Father, I speak encouragement and healing over the families, and I also declare restoration in the name of Jesus. You said in Your Word that all sickness is not until death. God, I ask that you strengthen the families to be able to accept Your will, and Father give them peace. Give them the peace that surpasses all understanding. I ask these and all blessings in thy precious son, Jesus' name, Amen!

Battle Behind the Sword

Chapter Six
Broken

"And I say unto you, whosoever shall put away his wife, except it be for fornication, and shall marry another, committeth adultery: and whoso marrieth her which is put away doth commit adultery"
(Matthew 19: 9).

After my father's death, Stan and I moved to Columbia, Missouri with me still fussing, and he was still cheating. Ironically, even through the fussing and cussing, I was becoming more spiritual. I know, that makes no sense! There was a spiritual transition that was taking place in some areas of my life, but not in my mouth. It's interesting to know that there can be spiritual growth in some areas, but not in all areas. I was learning and transitioning to the spiritual side of this Christian walk. All the while I was learning,

I was still bitter, rude, blunt, and dominant – basically, any negative force that was nameable. The problem at that time was fussing had become a normal way of life for me. I didn't feel as though I had a problem because I had become accustomed to it, and after all, my life had not been a walk in the park.

I loved the church, I loved Jesus, and Stan knew it. He knew that I was delighted that he was going to church all on his own. He was never the head of my life like I had envisioned in my mind. You know, the kind of head that would lead us into prayer together, lead us to church together. However, in my mind, I don't think the head that I had envisioned ever existed because my mind was full of confusion. Even if Stan carried "the head potential," I would have never known it, because all I did was fuss and complain. I had so much residue on me from the hurt of my past, it was just terrible. The funny thing is, I didn't even know it. One thing about changing who we are, *we* first must become a problem to ourselves. If our actions, ways, words, and character, never become a problem, then we will never fix it.

Anyway, the one thing I did take particular notice of was that he was going to church. I said to myself, "Well maybe he really got it."

We started going to the same church, but soon afterwards he started going to a different church. He was excited to go, but the one thing that I noticed was that he never asked me to go with him. Lying in bed one night and the Holy Spirit spoke to me and said, "He's seeing someone else, and he really is going to church, but the woman that he is seeing goes to the church with him."

I sat up on the bed, and thought, "That can't be right. No one in the church would be seeing a married man." Keep in mind that I was from the country and I had not yet realized that everyone did not think the way my family or myself, did. I would never sleep with a married man from the church, so surely another woman that is in the church would never sleep with a married man – especially if he was *in* the church. That was that country mentality, not realizing that I was not there anymore. "Linda," I thought. "You are not in the country anymore, and up here, they are a whole different breed of men and women."

Being this spiritual warrior (so I thought), the first thing I did was, started binding and rebuking what I heard, saying, "This thought is of the devil." I was so spiritually simple that it was pathetic. The reality was, I was not a spiritual warrior, I was a spiritual idiot.

I laid back down, this time I felt a tugging on my spirit. I started having visions of him and another woman. I thought that was the devil too, so I started praying against those thoughts. I bet God was saying, "This lady right here… I am probably going to have to send Gabriel the messenger, the prophets of old, the prophets of new, and the disciples, just so she will know that it is me, God that is tugging on her." Ha! Don't act like I'm the only one.

After a few minutes of no peace, I sent him a text message while he was at church and asked him was he cheating on me. He did not respond via text message but came home. He said the Lord said for him to come clean and stop lying to me. "Yes, I have been seeing someone." So I waited for him to finish, because if the Lord told you to come clean, then he also told you to repent as well. It was dead silence for a minute, so I understood that no apology, no repentance, no conviction, nothing was coming after that.

"Sooo, let me get this straight. So the Lord convicted you of lying, but he did not convict you of committing adultery?"

"The Lord has not convicted me of cheating!" he shouted.
I sat there in awe because I had never heard anything so stupid. Now why would God convict him of lying, but not convict him of adultery when both are sin?

"That is not how God operates. He doesn't convict you of one sin and not the other, so I question who was talking to you." I blurted out after I found my ability to speak again.

Listen, don't be fooled by the enemy into believing such foolishness. God does not - I repeat - God does not convict you of one sin and not the other. James 2:10 says, "For whosoever shall keep the whole law, and yet offend in one point, he is guilty of all." So, I highly doubt that the same God who inspired this scripture to be written is the same God that would convict you of lying and not convict you of adultery. Don't be deceived!

I was so torn up emotionally that I looked like the walking dead. I was totally zombified. I had no will, no emotions, no strength, I had nothing. One day I looked at myself in the bathroom mirror and I just cried and cried uncontrollably. I cried so hard that I got a headache. My eyes were bloodshot to the point where I could barely hold them open. Finally, the Spirit of the Lord spoke to me and said, "Wipe your tears."

"But God he cheated on me with no remorse."

"Is this what you truly want?" he asked.

"What do you mean, God?" I questioned once again.

"That man is downstairs talking to the woman that he has been cheating on you with, and he is talking to her in your house. Now again I ask, is this what you want? You are my daughter, and you don't come as number two to anyone."

"God, I thought you honored marriage." I cried as the tears began to flow once again.

"I do, but your husband doesn't."

"No, this is not what I want." I finally answered.

"Wipe your tears and tell him to leave."

"But God, I only make $10 an hour and I can't pay all of these bills on my own."

"Trust me," He said.

I pondered for a minute, wondering if this was really God talking to me, or if it was the pain of my heart speaking. So, I decided to go with believing that this is God talking to me. I said, "Okay, God," and I told Stan that he had to go, he had to leave my house.

Wait a minute! Is he asking me, where is he going to go? You know that I don't have anywhere to go? I simply looked at him and said, "You'd better call old girl and tell her you are homeless." I now know that it was God talking to me because in two weeks the Lord changed my position at my job. I can truly say that ever since then, He has supplied my every need.

My ex-husband and I had been together for seventeen years, and I felt like I was trash. I lost my womanhood through all of the hurt and pain he caused me. I lost my identity, I lost who Linda was. Funny thing, I was okay with splitting up. The truth was I was never in love with him. I was just comfortable with him and he was my security blanket. I didn't even love myself at that time. I was just *jacked* all up on the inside and thought I had everything going for me. Believe me, when God gets ready to take us to the next level, trust and believe He will show us, our old ugly selves. I thought that it was over. Stan was gone and was not coming back. But oh no, that would have been too easy. This man had the nerve to call me so that the other woman could go off on me. Yes, you heard me right. He called me so that she could give me a piece of her mind! Me, the wife of the man that she is sleeping with. I said to her, "Lady, you sleeping with my husband, and you're mad? How you can call yourself a Christian? It is women like you who are the reason that our churches are empty. Because you say you love God with your mouth, but your ways are of your real father, the devil. Hear me and hear me well - you have kids, and when you (the mother) step outside of the will of God willfully, you no longer have a spiritual covering. You are a sitting target for the enemy to do what he wants to do. Your sins will affect your children. When your kids come up sick, and the doctors don't know why, just know that it is because of the sins of their mother. Remember David and Bathsheba paid the ultimate price for the acts of their sin; they lost their son."

She continued to rant and rave about *my* husband! I was really stunned because, one, he called me for her, and two, I was the one that she was mad at, but she was sleeping with *my* husband. Church betrayal at its finest!

Well, Stan and his mistress decided that they were going to be a couple, so they went to get some spiritual counseling. The enemy had their minds believing that what they were doing was fine, and the church leaders were going to back them. Well were they wrong. The church bishop told him that he needed to get back to his wife.

Stan came back home. Two days before I went through his phone. I found a text message from his mistress saying that her daughter was in the hospital and the doctors could not figure out what was wrong with her. Her daughter had apparently been in there for four days, and her mother was scared. I just shook my head, because had I told her what might happen. She left him immediately.

Once again, he had nowhere to go, so he had to come back home, for the second time! I only allowed him back because his name was on the lease. Shortly afterward we got into an actual fistfight... Well, maybe I should say that I got into a fistfight and swung at him went straight to jail. *Yikes!* Needless to say, we ended up in divorce court. By that time, I was all cried out and didn't care about him. Goodbye!

I used to ask myself, did I run a good man off? The Lord answered, "No. What I have for you, is for you. Cheating on you and lying to you from day one, the relationship was bound for divorce court. What I have joined together, let no man put asunder." However, I do apologize for my actions. Although, I was totally blind to it, still, it was no excuse. I thought I was A-Okay! Again, I was *jacked* up, and there is no way that I could have been a wife to anyone. I was broken and didn't even know it. The funny part was, I was biblically smart but was spiritually ignorant.

The strange part about this whole thing was, I had intended to remain married to him. If he would have admitted his wrong, repented, and made up for the mistakes, I Linda would have stayed. Not because I loved him, but because I said, "Yes" to God through my marriage vows. About one year previous I had told my cousin, "I don't believe that I am carrying his rib, however, I will stay in the marriage because I made a vow to God to honor him until death do us part."

When God is truly a part of us, and there is nothing fake about our spirituality, then we will do our best to honor our commitment that we made to Him.

After the divorce, there were no hard feelings against Stan even though he was the one that wanted it, but I did a lot of repenting and forgiving myself for breaking my commitment to God.

One thing that I know now is that God knew that I was not perfect in the first place. He knew that I was going to come up short. He said in His word that all have sinned and come short of His glory. Jesus said that is why He went to the cross and carried our sins. The debt was paid through His bloodshed.

I would like to encourage each person reading this book not to let the enemy hold your past mistakes against you. Accept the fact that you messed up, repent (turn from the sin) and after you turn away from the sin, move on and do what God has called you to do.

Prayer for Broken Marriages

Dear heavenly Father, I ask that you come into these marriages that are broken and it seems like there is no hope. I ask that you heal the hearts of the husbands and wives, especially those that are trying to make it work for Your glory. I come against every Jezebel spirit that is trying to come in and destroy these marriages that have been ordained by You. God show Yourself mighty and stop them right where they are. I ask that You allow Your warring angels to slay them right where they stand. God, we ask that You blow a fresh wind on these Godly marriages and heal anything that is broken. In Jesus' name, Amen!

Chapter Seven
Raging Storms

"When He heard that, He said, this sickness is not unto death, but for the glory of God, that the Son of God might be glorified thereby" (John 11: 4).

So now I am in a new city, Columbia Missouri, all by myself and I am half way enjoying it in this area. I thought that up to this point in my life I had lost my mother, my father, my marriage, and almost lost my sanity, surely my struggles were over. God tested me, and I passed those tests with flying colors. I felt that I was in a good spiritual place because, after all that I had been through, I still loved God, and I still trusted Him. Yes, I may not have understood everything and the reasons I went through what I went through, but what I still knew is that I still loved God with everything that was in me.

I had praised my way through loss after loss, so in my mind, I was now a spiritual beast. I made it through the storms of life, and I still desired to remain steadfast and unmovable in my heavenly Father still trusting Him with my whole heart. What the enemy thought was going to break me, God allowed it to only strengthen me. I was not boastful or proud, but I was in a good spiritual place considering what I had been I had experienced.

Also, it appeared as though I was spiritually wise when I compared myself to the people in this area of Missouri. There were one or two things going on: either I was really deep and spiritual, or the church folks in this area were really spiritually ignorant.

After living in Columbia for a while, I learned that I was not spiritually deep, and the church folks here were spiritually ignorant; not all but most of the ones with who I came in contact. The foolishness in this area was so real that I was turned off from going to church. I knew that was a disaster that was waiting to happen, so I had to pick the best place to go for worship services, then I forced myself to attend. Where I came from, God is not something that you played with or took for granted. He is not something that you use to make you look good. He is not an entertainer. Little did I know; the church foolishness was the least of my worries.

My sister Michele and I worked at the same place for years. Everything was going well until I noticed that she was breathing hard and was getting out of breath quickly, but we attributed that to her being out of shape. Ha! I was out of shape too. We didn't think too much about it. Well, she had gotten to the point where it was getting harder and harder for her to breathe. We then chalked it up to maybe her getting a little chest cold. Over time, we noticed that she wasn't getting any better, but in fact, she was getting worse. At work, I would notice that she could not go up the stairs without having to stop, rest, and catch her breath. She then began to tell me how she felt. She said it felt like she was drowning in her own fluid (which is exactly what was happening, but we didn't know it), and trying to gasp for air. She was coughing non-stop. She was coughing to the point that she was getting on my nerves. I said, "Hey, we've got to do something about that cough."

We went to the doctor on several occasions, and they kept treating her for bronchitis. They gave her breathing treatments and steroids. One day Michele's cough had gotten so bad that her throat had become irritated, so we went to the doctor. He decided to do a chest x-ray. They discovered that she had an enlarged heart, and they sent her to a heart specialist. The steroids she'd been given had only exacerbated the problem because they made her heart muscle bigger. The doctor began to treat her for an enlarged heart, but her symptoms were steadily getting worse. One day while visiting her cardiologist, he told her that she had the heart of an eighty-three-year-old woman. He also stated that it was like her heart had suffered many heart attacks (but it hadn't).

She came to work with tears in her eyes and told me this devastating news. I remember sitting at my desk overwhelmed with so many emotions and with such devastation. I watched my sister as she walked away from my department. I felt the weight that she was carrying on her shoulders, so I got up and went to her department, found her and asked, "What else did the doctor say?" She answered, "The doctor said it doesn't look good for me." I did not think the news could be this devasting. I thought, Lord we just buried my dad a couple of years ago, and now this? When does it stop? Dang it! This family can't catch any breaks. I said to God, "What is it about this family that You keep us going through the fire?"

One day, she and I were going to the nail shop. When she got into my car, and I noticed that she was having trouble breathing. She leaned up against my dashboard. I began to pray hard. I said, "Lord, we are not from Columbia, so where can I take my sister for them to treat this heart condition?" The Lord put a certain hospital on my heart, so we headed in that direction after arguing with my sister about not going to the nail shop. I forced her to go to the hospital. I could do that since I was the one driving.

We got to the hospital, and Michele was not doing well at all. I was praying so hard for God not to take my sister. I truly don't think that I could have survived another death in my family, or another loss, I should say. I was praying, and I was keeping it one hundred percent with the Lord. I told Him, "Lord, she has five kids, and besides if something happened to her, guess who is next in line to raise them? Yep, me!" (Healing my sister and not taking her from me was something that I needed God to do because I did not want to have to care for five kids and two grandbabies.) Watch how the power of God moved in that situation.

While at the hospital, we both kept the faith. We encouraged each other. Keep in mind, all we knew was that she had a heart condition, and that was it. I sat there watching her be a trooper. She was still coughing non-stop, but she was in good spirits. You could tell her body was tired though. She was not able to breathe normally. She had to sit straight up in the bed to even breathe comfortably. Her breathing was heavy and hard. Meanwhile, I sat praying for God to show up. Luckily, there just so happened to be a doctor that was from out of town working at the hospital who specialized in heart conditions. He came in and saw her.

That doctor began to ask questions and ordered specific tests. Ten minutes later he came back with the diagnosis—the worst news of our lives. He told us that Michele had the worst case of congestive heart failure there was. He also told her that she needed a heart transplant immediately!

Talk about another blow—we were dumbfounded! Okay, here goes another battle, I thought. What kind of God am I serving? Or better yet, what is the point of this Christian walk? Am I holding to a faith that is non-existent? Or am I really not saved? Does God not like my family? What have we done to deserve this? All I know is something about this spiritual walk wasn't working for my family or for me.

For the first time in my life, all this Christian talk seemed pointless and empty. My question was, God, how much more do you want this family to suffer? I am not sure how much more "praises" I have in me. I'm not too sure how much "push" I got left in me. I'm not even sure if I want to continue to believe in this God that allows this much turmoil in my life. Yes, I know the Bible says that "a man born of a woman is of few days, but full of trouble," (Job 14:1). But that scripture was not supposed to apply to my sanctified and righteous self.

Nevertheless, I couldn't let my sister see me sweat too long. I took the news like a "gangsta," and I told my sister that we are going to get through this. When I got home, I let it all out. I cried like a baby. I cried asking God, "What are you trying to do to me? If you want me to kill myself, guess what? You are doing a really excellent job of getting me there." One thing that I learned through all my tears is that crying does not move the hand of God. After I got done crying and yelling at Him about how much He did not care about us, acting like Peter, who said, "Carest thou not that we perish?" Guess what? My sister still had congestive heart failure. My tears did not change the situation.

After I stopped having my pity party, I put on my spiritual war clothes. I cried, yelled, and told the devil with tears in my eyes, "I just buried my dad, and I am not about to bury my sister. If a fight is what you want Satan, then a fight is what you are going to get."

I went to work doing spiritual warfare. I got on the phone, and I found my sister a doctor in St. Louis who specialized in congestive heart failure - talk about a God-ordained situation! Dr. Geltman was and continues to be amazing. When my sister got to him, her heart infraction was at ten, and forty is normal. He immediately began to work by running specified tests developing a combination of drugs that would work for Michele.

At times the medicine would make her feel uncomfortable and she would call and let him know. He kept changing her medicine until he developed a system that worked. He then scheduled her for surgery to install a defibrillator in her chest. With all his efforts, Dr. Geltman was able to get my sister's heart infraction up to about twenty to twenty-five percent. We were excited about the progress that she was making and were grateful for the doctor that God lead us too.

As the years passed, after about the ninth year into her treatment, we notice that the medicines were not working like they used to. Michele began to fill up with fluid around her heart faster than her body could get rid of it. Dr. Geltman tried so many other alternatives. The treatments would work for a while and then they would stop.

After numerous treatments, and doctor visits, Michele had to have an L-VAD installed. An L-VAD is short for left ventricular assist device. It is an actual pump that is used for patients who reached the end stages of heart failure, and a heart transplant is the only option. They call it the bridge to the heart transplant. My sister joined a site where there were other L-VAD patients, some of their hearts are healing while the L-VAD did the actual work.

It has not been an easy journey, but my sister has been a soldier through it all. As of the writing of this book, we are enjoying life and trusting God, while we wait for a heart to become available, or while we wait for God to heal her original heart on this side of heaven. I've learned to be specific when asking something from the Almighty. I promise you that God is a keeper if you want to be kept. It is our desire to be kept by Him. I so wanted my sister to write this chapter of the book because I can't tell her story as she can. She said that she couldn't because the accounting class has her undivided attention. Oh, did I mention that Michele is now in college? God is amazing!

My sister knows that through it all, I have her back. She has her good days and bad days, but for the most part, we are beyond blessed. According to the doctors, she should have been dead a long time ago. They told us that most people don't live past thirty days in the condition that she started out in, but she had been walking around for seven months in that condition. The doctors were dumbfounded!

You can't tell me that God is not a keeper. He keeps us when we don't know that we need to be kept. Just in case anybody is wondering, it is your FAITH that moves the hand of God. Regardless of what we go through, God knows that we are human, and some blows happen in life which cause us to react out of the flesh, and that's okay. The main thing is, don't stay there. Sometimes you have to force your natural man to line up with your spiritual man.

For a long time, I questioned my spirituality, because I was hurting in my flesh. The way the religious people makes it seem, we are not supposed to cry, hurt, or feel emotions when we are going through things, but the devil is a liar! If you need to cry, cry! If you need to vent, vent! Don't keep that stuff inside, because if it stays too long, it will become spiritual cancer that takes over your body, thoughts, emotions, mind and your character. If you are hurting so bad that you can't get to the throne of God on your own, get to some sisters or brothers who can lift you up and petition the throne for you.

Yes, things happen. I don't care how strong you are, or how spiritual you are; there are some troubles in life that will knock the very breath that you breathe out of your soulful being, leaving you unable to function. It's a lie to believe that you won't go through anything because you are a child of the King.

One thing about me is, I'm a realist. I keep it one hundred! I call a spade a spade, and when I am hurting, I let God know that I am hurting. I can honestly say, that I was not happy about the things that I have endured. No ma'am, no sir! I am not happy at all.

However, I am glad that He went through it with me. I told Michele that I knew there would be days where she did not feel like worshipping or praising God. I said, "Don't worry about it. You have a baby sister who will go into the heavens on your behalf. Your sister has your back." I am my sister's keeper.

Prayer for a Sick Family

Dear heavenly Father, I petition the throne of grace on behalf of my sisters and my brothers who are dealing with a sickness. Father, we stand in need of Your healing power. Please send Your healing angels down to minister to our sick family members. Father, I ask that You strengthen anyone who is battling any sickness in his or her life. Father, I ask that You strengthen the loved ones who have to care for them. I ask that you lift them up where they may be torn down and strengthen them where they are weak. Father, we call on the Doctor of all doctors. We call on Jehovah-Rapha, the God of healing. Father, my sisters, and my brothers need You. God, we can't make this journey without You. Father, give them the grace to weather this storm, just as You did my sister and me. God, strengthen them to hold onto Your unchanging hand, and to stand on Your Word. You said that with Your stripes we are healed, and You are a God that You cannot lie. So, Father, I ask that You strengthen my brothers and my sisters to hold onto the faith. It is our faith that moves You God, not our tears, not our pity parties, but it's according to our faith. God, we thank You, that we have sent Your Word out, and it will accomplish just what it has set out to do and will not return to us void. In Jesus' name, Amen!

Chapter Eight
No Strength to Fight

"Though He slay me, yet will I trust Him: but I will maintain mine own ways before Him" (Job 13:15)

Oh, my God! This is the hardest one for me to do so I will make it brief because I still get emotional on this one. My family and I are extremely close, and God called my brother home in 2011. It was a major blow to us and very much unexpected. I can honestly tell you that this was the darkest, hardest, and loneliest time of my life. I thought I was not going to make it. I almost lost my mind. Talk about questioning God, being angry with Him, oh I was there. I had had it with this Christian journey. I thought, God what is the point? I probably was in a nonchalant state of mind for about two months, if not more. Although I was in a crazy place, I knew that I could not get through this catastrophe without the help of Jesus. I had to fast, pray, cry, vent, and stay in my Word every day. Even when the Word of God was not ministering to my spirit, and even when I didn't understand. I still had to work the Word into my life. I had been through too much to believe that I could get through this without Jesus. I had to force myself to stay in that Word every night. Yes, even with tears in my eyes, reading and crying myself to sleep, asking God, Why? Why? Why? Then I would say, "God, I know you don't make any mistakes." I had to constantly remind myself of the phrase, "God don't make no mistakes." I know that is improper English, but that is what I kept repeating.

Now that I look at everything soberly and how it happened, I can see that God was preparing my brother for his departure. Mike was at my house the weekend before he died. On that Saturday he came down from Iowa. We were laughing and cutting up as usual. My feet were hurting, and I was trying to get him to go to the store to get me something to rub on them. If anyone knew my brother, they knew that he would go, but I had to argue with him for about three hours before he just said, "Okay, okay, okay, I'm going." He was so agitated because he was trying to watch his cartoons, and of course, I was disturbing him. Before that, he and had I stayed outside talking about the goodness of Jesus for about four hours, which was something big for the both of us. That is a conversation that he and I have never, ever had. We have talked about God, but not the depths of the God, and not on a spiritual level.

This conversation about the Father, Son, and Holy Spirit was much different than before. He told me all about the people that he had done wrong. The people that he stole from, the people that he had robbed, and how he was going to go back to them to ask for forgiveness. There was one person that he talked about and said that once he comes into some money, he was going to pay them back. He never told me who that someone was, and that's okay because I know God count it as done. I was sitting there looking at the spiritual transition that was taking place in his life, that I never thought was possible. I was thinking, God are you changing my brother? Lord give me strength because I thought I would never see the day. This boy here was a drunk, a thief, a liar, and would rob you all while he was sleeping with your woman. That's why I said that conversation was HUGE!

Let me give you a little background on my brother. Mike inherited the demon of alcoholism from Momma. When she died, that demon took control of him. He was not strong enough to fight it, and the truth is, he liked to drink. Let's just be real about the situation - there are some sins that we like, and we really don't want to stop doing. Well, alcohol was his.

I will never forget. One day we were at home, and Mike and Momma had a huge argument. That was typical in my home—my brother arguing with my mother, my father arguing with my mother. (FYI-If a young man sees his father disrespecting his mother, chances are the son is going to disrespect the mother as well). Michele and I were the peaceful ones of the family. Anyway, Momma always kept a pistol and wooden stick with his name on it. These weapons were specifically designed for Michael Alvin Jr. just in case he wanted to try her. Every time he and Mom would get into a fight, she would not hesitate to go upside his head. Once she told him, "I will do life in prison before I let you run over me in my own house. The house that I pay the bills in? Boy, I will kill you. I brought you into this world, and rest assured I will take you out. Try me if you want to!" Now my mother was from Detroit, and given her track record, I believed her, and Mike did too.

It never failed, every time after Momma and Mike would fight, and she would put him out of the house. This was the strange part, she then would go into her bedroom and pray for him. I would always listen to her. She would ask God to take care of her son. At that time, I was maybe ten years old. I was thinking, it seems pointless to put him out and then go and pray for him, but I get it now. Shortly after that, Mike moved to Michigan where he tried to burn up his girlfriend and went straight to prison.

Guess what happened? Momma died. Yes, she died while he was in prison, so he never got to say he was sorry, he never got a chance to say, "Momma, I love you." He had to live the rest of his life with that dark cloud of un-forgiveness over his head. That is what led to an increase in his drinking, and his manipulation of women.

One day, he and I were sitting in Charleston, Missouri and we were talking. I was just really trying to get an understanding of his thought process and why he thought the way he thought because his thinking was warped. After we got deep into a deep conversation, he broke down crying to me and said, "The only woman that I ever trusted, God took her from me," meaning my mother. He said, "That is why I treat women the way that I do because I don't trust them." Mike had no problem disrespecting women. He said whatever he felt, and whatever came to his mind. He would call a woman out of her name, slap her if he felt like it, and curse her out whenever he wanted to. He absolutely had no respect for women that were not his family. After that conversation, I understood him a little better. I'm not saying that I agreed with him, but now I understood why he did the things that he did. Now that I am older, I can see the damage done to him through Momma's death. I am sure that most of the pain came from the last time he saw Momma, he was cussing her out and threatening to beat her down. The truth of the matter is, my brother was scared to love. He was scared to give his heart to any women because, in his mind, she would leave him. Just like Momma did.

A lot of times we don't want to accept the realization of the deep-rooted pain that people are carrying around. The magnitude and the depth of the pain will hinder people emotions, their ability to love and their ability to be loved. This is more commonly seen in men than it is women. The reason is that women often will express their emotions and their feelings to other women. Most women don't have a problem with expressing how they feel. For men, on the other hand, it is not that easy.

I believe that this happens because men are raised never to show weakness when they are hurting. Think about it, if you are raising a boy child and he falls and hurts himself, the first thing you say to him is, "You'd better not cry. I ain't raising no sissy." They live with the notion that, if I show that I am hurting, then I am acting like a sissy and I ain't no sissy. In a sense, we have trained them that when they are hurting never to show emotions. We have trained to keep it to yourself and walk the pain out without showing any signs that you are hurting. This is why sometimes women feel like we will get better results from talking to a brick wall because this affects their ability to communicate like men.

The Tuesday before Mike's death, I had a dream that I had gotten killed. I have had dreams before of maybe falling off a cliff, but never hitting bottom. This dream was much different. In this dream, I was dying. Like, transitioning to the other side. I remember what my exact prayer was as I was dying in the dream. I said, "Lord, I pray that I have lived a life that was pleasing in Your sight. Please welcome me into your Kingdom." As I was saying those words, I noticed that I was laying there in a pool of blood, because in my dream I had been shot by someone that I knew. This dream would not leave my spirit. The next day, the group that I used to sing with had rehearsal, and I shared the dream with them. That's how I knew that God was trying to tell me something, because I was still thinking and talking about the dream, and what took place. I could not shake it. I remember after sharing the dream with them, we sang a song, and my cousin who is spiritual said, "We've got go back to this dream." We talked about the dream some more. This was on Wednesday.

That following Thursday - I remember like it was yesterday. I was at work when the phone call came. There was a lady on the other end, let's just call her "Samantha." She told me that Mike was not breathing and that the paramedics were outside in my yard working on him! Well myself being in a spiritual place, I said, "Okay, I'm praying and believing God." She said, "No, you don't understand, Mike is not breathing." I said, "I'm still trusting God." I went home immediately where we got the phone call that he had passed. At the time, I didn't know what I was feeling. It was a combination of hurt, pain, a sense of loss, the emptiness, the coldness, but mainly confusion. I know that it was a pain like no other. I had never felt such loss before in my life, and I had been through a lot. Now, everything that I had been through seemed so insignificant compared to this pain. The pain of losing my sibling was much different than the pain of losing my parents. I can't explain it. Maybe because I was much younger when I lost my mother, so maybe that is why the pain was different. I know that with my father, he had a stroke, so the possibility of death was there. Maybe because knowing that death was a possibility, it helped lighten the blow for when death showed up. But with my brother, this pain was in the gut-wrenching depths of my soul. I don't know how to cope, function, think, or move from this place. This death had me paralyzed to the reality of life…umm, I literally could not move!

As the news made its way through our home, I remember the screams and the whaling that echoed through the house. My sister and I were trying to console the kids. Everyone was just hugging and crying. For once in my life, I said, "God, I ain't gonna make it. God if you are trying to take me out, or if you are trying to make me lose my mind, then I will say to you Almighty God, MISSION ACCOMPLISHED." There were people just calling, and calling, and calling, to see if it was true. After talking to them, there were even more screams coming through the phone.

Mike's death was the very first time that I thought my life was over. I was fussing the entire time; I said "God, you have taken my brother and my friend. God, Mike was changing spiritually, so why would you take him from me? My sister, the kids, and I never got to enjoy much of the new Mike. The spiritually changing Mike." I felt like giving up my faith, and every piece of belief in God that I had. I truly believed that my spiritual walk was over.

During this time, I had to mask the pain. I couldn't let anyone know that I was not a spiritual soldier and that I wanted to tell God a thing or two, or three. So, I did just what I do best. In the darkest hour of my life, I went and sought the face of God. Even though I was mad at God, I was numb to what had happened, I didn't want to hear about Jesus, but I needed to talk to Him. Yes, through it all, I still chose to seek the Lord because that is all I knew to do. I remember turning to the wall, tears streaming down my face, heart tore completely up, and I started singing. "I love You, Lord, and I lift my voice - to worship You, Oh, my soul, rejoice. Take joy, my King - into what you hear - let it be a sweet, sweet sound in Your ear." My voice was cracking because of the pain, but I had to push the worship out. And to be honest, I didn't mean the words that I was singing, but I kept singing until I did. I was reminded of the scripture that says after David lost his son, he went and worshipped:

> But when David saw that his servants whispered, David perceived that the child was dead: therefore, David said unto his servants, Is the child dead? And they said He is dead. Then David arose from the earth, and washed, and anointed himself, and changed his apparel, and came into the house of the Lord, and worshipped: then he came to his own house; and when he required, they set bread before him, and he did eat. Then said his servants unto him, What thing is this that thou hast done? Thou didst fast and weep for the child, while it was alive; but when the child was dead, thou didst rise and eat bread," (2 Samuel 12: 19-21).

My brother died on a Thursday, so we decided to go to church that Sunday. I knew what to do. I had been in this dark place before. I knew that I had to worship. I was thinking, how in the world am I going to get this worship out?

That Sunday, the Bishop said, "I am surprised to see you all here." I said, "My circumstances do not change my position with Christ." Although my words sounded strong, I was really jacked up on the inside. However, my sister, my cousins and I praised God like there was no tomorrow. The spirit of the Lord overtook us, and I needed the spirit of the Lord to overtake me. Although I was confused in my flesh, I knew what I needed to do in my spirit.

I believe that when tragedies hit us, it's easy to get lost in the pain and the hurt. Sometimes, we get so lost that we lose focus and forget about the spiritual weapons that God has provided so that we can be equipped. When we forget about those weapons, and we get lost so deep in the pain, that is when the enemy comes in, and that is where the spirit of depression, oppression, suppression, anxiety, fear, doubt, and all sorts of negative emotions, set in and rest upon us. David reminds us that even in our darkest hour, we still must worship. Sometimes we don't understand why things happen, and that is okay. The key is not to dwell on the "whys of life." Meaning, don't stay in a place of questioning 'Why did this happen?' or 'Why did that happen?' The beauty of worship is we can worship knowing that we are welcoming God's presence and peace. Contrary to what we may be feeling at the time when we are hurting, God's presence is where we need to be. We need to be at His feet, and we need to do whatever we need to do to get there and not leave until our souls find peace.

When we ask God *why*, or when we demand a reason for Him doing what He has done, one thing that I have learned is that sometimes God will reveal to us His reasoning's and there are sometimes He will not. To the believer, our focus must be, "God, I don't understand everything, but I trust You." I'm not saying that this is an easy task because it is not, but if you want to come out of hurt a spiritual warrior, then know that worship and complete trust in Him is necessary.

When I came home from church, I realized that I was in a fight for my sanity. The enemy was trying his best to come against my mind and my thoughts. Oh yes, even when I was worshipping the enemy was still trying to take my mind. Many people believe that when we speak the Word of God over our situation that the enemy stops attacking. Yes, the Bibles does say, "at the name of Jesus the devil has to flee," but it did not say that he would not come back. So guess what that means? You must continually and constantly speak the Word of God over your life.

Satan will do his best work when you are in a dark place, and hear me when I say, I was in a dark place. I had to have spiritual talks, and conversations on a constant basis. Sometimes the conversation was with other people, and sometimes the conversation was with me. I don't care what people say; sometimes we have to speak to ourselves while in pain. I believe that it is very beneficial to talk to ourselves because the more we can hear ourselves with positive affirmations, the more we will believe what we say and hear. We just need to make sure that we are decreeing and declaring the Word of God in our lives.

This situation was so spiritually sensitive that I would not allow any negativity in my ears. This is one of the places where I learned how to do spiritual warfare against the enemy. I heard all sorts of negativity from the enemy like, "If God loves you, why would He allow this? Ha, you have lost your mother and your father and now this? Not to mention your sister needs a heart transplant and now this? Also, didn't your husband just leave you and now this? What kind of God is this?" I told the enemy, "Those are good questions, but no matter what I go through Satan, I will never bow down and worship you."

During this dark period of my life, I am not going to lie, there were times I told God, "If this is what ministry is all about, then you can keep it, I don't want it." I told the Lord, "I'm good on that." Then there were times I asked Him, "Why did you choose me for this ministry mission? I didn't ask for this, heck I didn't even ask to be born. You mean to tell me, out of everything that I have gone through, and out of everything that you have allowed in my life, you still want me to go out and minister your Word? God, obviously your Word is not doing anything for me, but causing havoc and chaos? Nah, I'm good."

The truth is, it is the Word of God that actually kept my sanity. It was the Word of God that strengthened me to push through the pain. Mike's death was the death that nearly took me out, but the worship that I forced out of my mouth, and out of my belly would NOT allow it too.

I want to encourage whoever is dealing with a loss of a loved one; I want you to know that your worship is vital in that place. Your worship is a must, even if you don't feel like it, you have got to force it out. Even when you don't think that the worship is doing you any good, you must worship anyway. When you put worship in the atmosphere, it causes a shift in the spiritual realm. Every area that enemy was trying to bind you up in, he must let you go. Worship keeps depression away, worship keeps doubt and fear away. You may even feel a spirit of heaviness on you, but when you worship, the spirit of heaviness must leave in Jesus name. Keep on worshipping, even if you have to turn on your worship music and just let it soak you. DO IT!

Prayer for Those Who Are Confused

Heavenly Father, I come to you on behalf of my brothers and my sisters, who have been hit by the troubles of life to where they feel like they have lost their way. I ask that You invade their minds and their spirits, and fill them with Your love, Your joy, and Your peace. Father, I ask that You give them a spirit to rest in You. Father, sometimes things happen in life that we don't understand, but help us not to focus on the pain, but to focus on Your Word, and help us to stand on Your promises. Lord, I ask that where there may be confusion and deep wounds, I ask that You send Your ministering angels to help soften the blow. Father God, I come against every spirit of depression, confusion, misunderstanding, and defeat, in the name of Jesus. Father, we take authority over the enemy in Jesus' name. Father, I ask that You strengthen my brothers and my sisters to say, "I don't understand this season of my life, and yes it hurts, but God, I trust you." We ask these, and all blessings, in thy son, Jesus' name, Amen!

Battle Behind the Sword

Chapter Nine
This is Too Much God

"Purge me with hyssop and I shall be clean: wash me, and I shall be whiter than snow" (Psalms 51:7)

As of the writing of this book, I am forty-two years of age, and I can look back over my life and see how God was preparing me for ministry work in His Kingdom. Yes, many of the lessons that I went through were hard lessons. The truth is that God Himself can only teach some lessons. When He teaches, He *really* teaches us. We have no other choice but to recognize that it was Him all along. When He begins to maneuver in our lives, He takes us through the process of purging.

The process of purging is and has been pure agony to my flesh. Many times, people don't understand what goes on behind the scene when it comes to true ministry. Note: I said *True Ministry*, not a ministry of performance. Having a true ministry does not mean that our lives have been perfect and that we have always had it all together. As a matter of fact, it's quite the opposite. When God is preparing us for ministry, we have got to get ready to go to some places that we are not going to like or understand. Get ready for people to hurt you and betray you when you have not done anything wrong. For true ministry to take place in our lives, the purging process is mandatory. We must go through the harshness of purging so that we can get to that place where God has called us.

Most people want the progress, but no one wants to go *through* the process. I can honestly say, I didn't want the process or the progress, but since I have been chosen by God, and called by Him, I didn't have a choice in the matter. When God has us on assignment, we might as well get ready, because He is in control of our every move. One thing that I have learned through this entire journey is that God always gets His way; voluntarily or involuntarily.

I am going to be as honest as I can and as real as I can; the process of purging is terrible. Yes, I said it; it is terrible. The definition of purging means to get rid of whatever is impure or undesirable. Because we are born in the flesh, Paul tells us that nothing good comes from the flesh. Our flesh is corrupt, so, therefore, a hard-spiritual cleansing must take place in our life, and it is very much necessary for ministry. When we say, "Yes, Lord, I will go and preach your gospel, I will say what you want me to say, I will do what you want me to do, I will go where you want me to go, my soul says, Yes!!" Sounds familiar, huh? Sounds good, huh? Sounds sure, huh? Let me help you understand what you said "yes" too. You just said yes to heartache, heartbreak, suffering, loneliness, coldness, betrayal, etc. You get the point. Get ready, because misery for ministry is on the way.

Speaking of ministry, some people confuse ministry with preaching. People think because the prophet Isaiah said, "Lord send me, I'll go," that he was talking about preaching a sermon. Umm… NOPE! But, that is entirely another book. Ministry means to serve God at all costs. To translate what Isaiah said, he meant, "Lord, you can use me for your glory, whether it be through sickness, through despair, and sometimes even through death. It's whatever you choose, Master." We no longer belong to ourselves. It is literally in Him that we move, breathe, and have our being. The question is, will your "yes" still be a "yes"? We need to be careful quoting scriptures of which we do not have the full understanding.

When it comes to the purging process, *everything* that is not of

God that has attached itself, guess what? It must fall away, and only God can do that. Let me go a little deeper with this. I am going to speak from a woman's standpoint. Here is a revelation that God gave me as I wrote this book. When I say everything, we are talking about everything. Yes ladies, every man that we have ever laid with, and who has released himself in us, we must be stripped of them - not only them but every demonic spirit they carried - they released them in us, too. So now, God not only has to purge us of our issues and spirits, but He has to purge us of the issues of the men that we laid with, too.

Let's do some math. Let's say I have suffered rape, molestation, drug addictions, loss, betrayal, hurt, pain, lust, confusion, fornication, and have been with about fifteen men (this is just an example). Then, the men that I have slept with had also suffered loss, molestation, or their mothers did not want them. Additionally, each one of them had slept with about ten to fifteen women each (remember, all their partners had demons too). That means God had a lot of stripping and purging to do on me. Now, with these figures, I understand why purging hurts so bad. Look at what God has to purge/strip from us! Just look at everything that has attached itself to us that is not of God. Good God Almighty, Lord help us today!

Purging is a very crucial part of becoming a disciple of Christ.

Purging gets us prepared for the next level of spirituality. When we are true to God and serious about ministry, then a harsh cleansing is what we will experience. It's like a spiritual detox, which means everything that is not of God, or everything that is a spiritual hindrance must be removed. Yes, even if we are carrying things that are weighing us down—it has to go. Yes, even if it means separation from someone that we love. To minister effectively, we must be purged. We must go through the fire so that we can reach someone else. In other words, I can't teach you if I can't reach you.

It's easy to tell someone how to deal with their problems, or how we would handle the situation, but we are not them. I heard a young lady tell a minister about what she had been through as a child, and how it affected her mentally, spiritually and emotionally. The conversation went on, then the minister proceeded to tell the young lady that her struggles should never affect her, nor should it affect her spirituality. The minister proceeded to tell that young lady that she has to give that hurt to God. My response to the young lady was, "You should have asked her (the minister) 'are speaking from experience? Or, are you speaking because someone told you that you were a minister?' Because minister or not, if someone has not been raped or molested by a family member, then they can't tell another individual how to react to the pain that they feel. We can guide and instruct them on how to handle their emotions according to the word of God, but we cannot tell them that how they are feeling about the situation is wrong. People are affected differently because no one is made up of the same spiritual DNA.

This is why purging is so critical for ministry. It forces us into the fire, and the fire is purifying us as we go through it. The truth is there are some bondages that we carry, and we don't even realize that they are hindering our movements. The fire is freeing and removing any bondages that have us bound, just as it did with the Hebrew boys. The truth is there are some bondages we carry that we don't even realize they are there, so going through the fire is a must. Just like Hebrew boys, the fire cannot consume us as long as the Son of Man is in the fire with us. The fire has been instructed by God only to consume the things that bound us. To be honest, coming from a minister who was anointed and appointed by God, I hated the purging process!

I went through some things that I (Lady Linda) took myself through, but that was part of the purging process, as well. It's called trial and error. After all of this, I was betrayed by someone that I truly loved. During this difficult time, I allowed God to put me in the belly of the whale. It felt just like the belly of the whale - surrounded by guts, blood, foul odor - agony was all around Lady Linda. Guess what I told God? "God this is not what I signed up for." Then I began to question my own spirituality. I said, "God, I am reaping some things that I did not sow." I did a thorough investigation of my life, and I became a little puzzled. I said, "God, I have not been perfect, but I have never treated people the way that I am being treated right now." Again, I found myself seeking God in the midst of the pain. The more I stayed on my face seeking Him, the more He began to reveal some His mysteries to me. He also began to give me spiritual wisdom. He showed me why the pain was necessary, and how it will benefit the Kingdom for ministry. If I could be real about the whole thing, I didn't care a thing about ministry while I was going through this process. God said the pain was all for ministry purposes. All I knew was, I didn't sign up for such madness, for such pain, for such hurt, and come to think about it, nor did I sign up for ministry. I said, "If this is ministry God, you can keep it. I'm good and thank you for considering me to do work in your Kingdom, but this isn't for me. Don't worry, imma still be saved, sanctified, and filled with the Holy Ghost sitting right here watching *Lifetime*. According to the scripture, I will still make it to heaven when I die. Let's just leave it at me being saved and staying saved; I don't need any spiritual extras. Yes, I still love You Lord with all my heart. This is just too much pain for my spirit."

There were so many nights that I laid in the bed asking God, "Do

You even like me? Why are you allowing all this pain if you love me so much? I don't care what you say, God, this is not love." Maybe I am not the only one who has gone through this. The purpose of this book is to let people know about what goes on behind the word that they hear being ministered. It's about me, and *My Battle Behind the Sword!* It is about my struggles and my truths. Thumbs up to those who went through the purging process and never questioned God. God Bless you! Because that sure was not me.

This is the realness on how God deals with us as He prepares and strengthens us for ministry. This is the ugly truths that people don't see and the ugly truths that others don't know about. On Sunday mornings, people are accustomed to hearing a good power filled, Holy Ghost anointed message, not knowing about the war that's going on with God behind closed doors. A lot of wars are not meant to be shared with everyone, but God has released me to share some of my truths. I just need people to understand that there is a purging process for ministry and it is REAL. The question is, can you handle it? When God gets to purging your flesh, can you handle it? When He leads you to the Red Sea, and Pharaoh is behind you, can you still handle it? Or, will you give up and go back to where you started? Will you punk out on God? Will your "yes" still be a "yes"?

Let's talk about the weak ones for a minute. There are some spiritual punks in the ministry. Yes, because the pain got so unbearable, people have punked out on God. I have heard them denounce God and His very existence, all because things got rough, or things didn't go their way. Well, this is why we can't walk this journey alone. We need to have some prayer warriors in our corner that will not let us give up on God. They will keep us lifted before the throne of Grace, even when we can't get there ourselves. Yes, there were times that I didn't feel like praying, I didn't feel like reading any scriptures, and I didn't want a scripture read to me either. I didn't want to hear anything about Jesus, all because I was mad at God. But my prayer warriors did not allow me to give up, they did not allow me to give in, and nor did they allow me to give out. They prayed me through it; they encouraged me through it. Listen, if our friends are not speaking life into us, if they are not encouraging us, if they are not seeking God on our behalf, if they are not giving us wise counsel, then they are not our friends. Sorry that I had to be the one to relay this vital piece of information.

Now, I understand that during the purging process there will be those who question, or assume they know the reasons for such a painful journey. Just like they with did Job. His friends questioned him and assumed that he had done wrong and that is why he was going through so much turmoil. Therefore, we have to react like Job; he told them, "I don't need any of you questioning me, and I don't owe any of you any explanations. I am just as spiritual as you are, so you are in no place to try and judge me."

The truth is, at the time that we are going through the purging process, we don't even know why we are going through the troubled water ourselves. Most of the time God has not revealed that the pain is for ministry, and Kingdom building. He just sends us through the fire. Sometimes He wants to see what we are made of. Can you handle the fire? Many people have said "yes" to ministry, and soon as the fire got hot, they were gone. Many people have said "yes" to God, "yes God I need you to lead me, I want you to lead me," and soon as He starts leading through the fire, they change their minds. My question is once again, "Do you know what you are saying YES to?" I will say this for the rest of my life, "You are not saying 'yes' to preaching a sermon."

When the purging process starts, God is saying that we must rid ourselves of everything that is tainted or contaminated with sin. It's time to get rid of all those spirits that have found rest inside of our hearts. See that is where God wants to reside, and He can't get there if that space is occupied. Let me be real, with purging come great pain and losses – including friends and relationships. When God invades our spirits and begins the process of purging in the depths of our souls, rest assured that He is getting rid of every nasty thing that we allowed to attach to us either internally, or externally. Whether it entered in through sex, through our hearts, through our minds or our eyes, however, it got in, just know that it's getting ready to come out. It is a very painful process. Look at it this way, everything that we have come to know, and have become comfortable with, everything that makes us the sinners we are, they're getting ready to be removed. Yes, the Master is getting ready to perform a spiritual surgery. He is getting ready to cut and clean us from the inside out. There is no medicine to ease the pain, we have got to feel every cut, every stick, every tug and every pain.

I love how God purges us of the simple things like how we dress, or what we watch on TV. During the process, our desires will begin to change; our thought process will begin to change as well. For example, in this season of my life, I don't like for my arms to show when I am in the pulpit or while I am ministering. I can remember a time where I didn't even think about anything like that. See after surgery, God will give you a new walk, a new talk, and a new way of seeing things. Understand, the purging process will only work if we allow it to work. We must do our part, as well. For example, someone who is an adulterer and is trying to be purged from that adulterous spirit, does not need to be hanging around other adulterers. Likewise, if someone is an alcoholic, then they don't need to be around alcohol or friends that consume alcohol. Remember I said, there are going to be some people that you are going to have to let go; family is not exempt. This is the place where God really begins to teach, instruct, guide, and test us. Whatever our issues may be, this is where we must learn to deny our flesh and bring it under subjection to the Spirit that is now dwelling within us. Here comes the battle!! Before, we were allowing the flesh to do whatever it wanted to do, and we were giving it whatever it desired. We were succumbing to those fleshly desires that felt good - now, it's a different ball game. We must make that nasty flesh succumb to the holy nature of God. This means not giving the flesh what it wants, or desires. Tragic!! The Apostle Paul talks about the Spirit warring against the flesh. THIS THING IS REAL YALL!!!

One of my experiences while going through my period of purging is as such - I loved men as you could tell, but when I answered the call of God, I had to be purged of them – not only them but every demonic spirit they carried. It was a very hard process to go through, but it can be done. The question is, "Do you love God more than you love your sin?" The Bible says in II Corinthians 5:17, "Therefore if any man is in Christ, he is a new creature: old things have passed away and behold all things have become new."

After acknowledging the call of God to ministry, those who are chosen need to know that it's going to get rough. As a matter of fact, the pain will almost seem unbearable, and seemingly unnecessary. Get ready to feel lonely, confused, angry, bitter, betrayed, disappointed, and everything else that doesn't seem spiritual. Just know that it truly is working together for your good. I know that at times it doesn't seem like it, and it sure doesn't feel like it - take it from someone who has been purged and is still being purged. Remember the bible says, "The race is not given to the swift or the strong, but he that endures to the end." The question is, "Can you handle the process?" If you can't handle the purging process, then you may want to re-seek the face of God regarding ministry. Why? Because true God breathed deliverance, God-breathed anointing, and God-breathed ministry, is all made manifest in the purging. No purging means no deliverance; no deliverance means no anointing; no anointing means no ministry. Are you ready? Whatever you do, don't say "yes" to ministry because it looks good. I am telling you the truth that no one else wants to tell you. During the purging process, will your "yes" remain a "yes"?

Prayers for Purging Strength

Dear heavenly Father, I stand in on behalf of my brothers and my sisters who are going through the purging process. God, sometimes it feels so lonely, and the pain seems unbearable, but God we are looking to You for strength. Right now, we need strength to hold on and to hold out. God, we know that we picked up some things that are not of You, and those things have to come out of us. Often, the pain gets so bad that we want to throw in the towel and give up, but God, we will keep looking to the hills from where comes our help, and we know that all our help comes from you. God, we realize that You have charged us with an assignment, and we accepted the charge. We cannot carry this mantle in our own strength, but through Your help, we can carry the assignment out. We come against the spirit of doubt, fear, and confusion, through the anointing of the Holy Ghost. We declare and decree that we will not get weary in well doing. We take authority over our minds and over our spirit right now. David said, wait on the Lord, and He will strengthen thine Heart. God, we don't understand much about the process, but God, we trust you. We trust that You know what we need to keep, and we trust that You know what we need to get rid of. Lord, we ask that You don't move our mountains, but God we ask that You strengthen us to climb them. Lord, don't allow us to focus so much on the pain that we forget about Your promise, but let us remember that "All things work together for the good of them that love the Lord, and are called according to His purpose." God, we will always be careful to give You the honor, the praise, and the glory, in Jesus' name. Amen!

Chapter Ten
It's all Good

"And we know that all things work together for the good to them that love God, to them who are called according to His purpose" (Romans 8:28)

The above scripture can easily be misinterpreted or misunderstood. The scripture specifically says that if you are called to be beneficial to the Kingdom, then everything that you are going through, or have been through, is working for your good. Yes, even the things that you have allowed yourself to get in. Believe it or not, that too is working for your good. The scriptures never said that what you would be going to go through, would be all good or even feel good. It said these life events are working for your good. Sometimes, we go through things that hurt us to the core, but if we believe God and take Him at His Word, then it has got to work out for our good. God understands that we are human that we are not going to always handle the pain correctly, but He is just to forgive us for our shortcomings. Jesus went to the cross because He already knew that we were going to mess up and that we were not going to be perfect. Here is a secret for you, God does not judge based how many times we messed up, He judges according to our hearts' intent. This why God doesn't want anyone else to judge us, because man judges the outer action, but God judges the heart of a man. That should have freed somebody right there.

One thing that we must learn to do is, while we are going through the fire, we must make it a point to work the Word over our lives. We must understand that God loves us and that His Word will not return unto Him void. We must speak His Word over ourselves and over our situations. There have been times where I have been hurt so bad that I have had to tell myself with tears in my eyes that it's working for my good. "God, I don't understand it, but it's working for my good." Sometimes I say, "God, it sure doesn't feel good, but according to your Word it's working for my good. I know that you are going to get the glory out of this situation somehow".

See God wants our problems to push us closer to Him. He wants us to be strengthened by our problems. After all, that is what storms are designed for. When we go through trials and tribulations, we are to seek the rest of God. When we are frantic, anxious, and our mind is everywhere, we cannot hear from Him. We already know that no one can get through to us when our minds are in a confused place. This is when we are to seek the wisdom of God. He said in the book of James, "If any man seeks wisdom let him ask."

Wisdom will give you spiritual insight of the storm. Spiritual insight is seeing the little picture at first, however, the more we seek God's wisdom we will begin to see with intensity, and He will begin to show us the bigger picture. If we seek our own human wisdom, this will lead us deeper into the storm because now we are trying to figure it out so we can try to fix it. So we must then seek instructions from God. If we don't seek instructions from Him, then I can guarantee that we will not handle this storm right. We will not work the storm the way God intended, but we will work the storm according to what we think, and how we understand the situation. The Bible clearly tells us in the book of Proverbs to lean not to our own understanding. (Side note: I, Linda will lean to my own understanding "QUICKLY"). If we don't work the storms right, the enemy will use them to distract us from focusing on God's purpose and His plan for our lives.

Every believer has a decision to make. Are we going to let our problems strengthen us and push us closer to God, or are we going to let them detour us and put us on a downward path? Let's look at the outcome of both decisions. Choosing to allow the storms to push us closer to Christ, then we are going to come out with peace. Choosing to allow the storm to push on the downward slope, then we are going stay in the storm, and will be bitter, angry and mad at the world over something that we cannot change.

We must also learn to rest in God. There is nothing like having that peace that surpasses all understanding operating in your life, while a volcano has irrupted all around. Now peace is not something that comes all of the time naturally. There are some cases where the Bible teaches us that we must pursue peace. Yep, sometimes we are going to have to work at finding the peace of God.

We cannot at any time underestimate the enemy's tactics that he uses on us. Right when it seems like we may see some light in a dark tunnel, here comes the enemy throwing another weapon at us, and now suddenly it is dark again. However, the key is to keep believing, keep trusting, and keep resting in God. The number one thing that the enemy tries to invade is our thought process. We must protect our minds at all costs. Satan knows that if he gets control of our minds, then he has control of us. You must protect your mind with everything that is within you.

Sometimes I like to write "in" the moment because I want every person reading this book to understand that the enemy has not stopped coming at me. Just because I have overcome some of my trials, does not mean that he has surrendered. Even as I sit here writing this chapter, I feel a weight of heaviness in my spirit. It's like something is trying to invade my inner courts, and we all know that only God can dwell there. I just need you to know that "it's all good," and to God be the glory of whatever it is. One thing that I am certain of is that I will continue to fight the good fight of faith.

As I look back over my life and see all that has happened and all that I have gone through, I would be lying to you if I said I can see the good in everything that I have encountered. I do know that no matter the magnitude of the pain, somehow or another, it all still has worked and is working together for God's Glory. Now there are some things that I can see the good in and how it has benefited, but not all things. For example, if my father would not have passed away, then I would have never moved from Poplar Bluff, Missouri. Why? Because my father was a stubborn man, and he loved living in the Neelyville/Poplar Bluff area. He would have never moved, and I would have never left him.

However, because of his death, I was able to move to Columbia and get hands-on spiritual training about the assignment that God has me on. I like to say that my hometown is where I learned the Bible, but Columbia is where I learned through hands-on training. Columbia is where I learned the spiritual side of or should say, this where I learned to operate in the spiritual realm. Contrary to what people might say, you can have Bible knowledge and still be spiritually ignorant. It doesn't do any good to learn the Word of God, and not know how to operate it in your life.

Another example is if my mother would have still been alive, or lived longer, that spirit of lust would have matured in my spiritual being. The truth is, I'm not sure that it would have ever left me. I do believe the fight to do warfare against that lustful demon would have been harder than it was. Therefore, it would have handicapped me or disabled me from working for the Kingdom. When God has placed us here on earth for an assignment, we need to remember and just know that He will remove whoever, and whatever that needs to be removed for us to do His work. Kingdom work trumps everything. It trumps our fears, our emotions, our feelings, and it even trumps what we think. Just like I have been trying to move from Missouri for what seems like to be forever, but I can't go anywhere because God has put me in somewhat of spiritual restraint until I finish this assignment here in this area. The Bible teaches, "A man's heart plans his ways; but the Lord directs his steps," (Proverbs 16:9). In other words, man makes his own plans, but God is going to order his steps in the way and where He wants them to go. This scripture cracks me up because we literally don't have a choice, but to do what God said to do.

Also, all of these trials have taught me not to be judgmental, but to seek God for instructions on how to minister to a specific individual; regardless of what sin that person may be involved in. One thing that I have learned is that I cannot expect people to handle a storm the way I would. When people are going through things, it's easy to say what he or she should do according to my thoughts, my spiritual being, what I have been taught, or the way I see it, but that is the way that I see it. That doesn't mean that is the way that everyone else sees things. A young lady told me one day, "Linda, your common sense and my common sense are two different things." That ministered to my soul, and it helped me to see things from a different perspective. I believe that when we provide spiritual counsel from that place of, "the way I see it," or "you should have done it this way," I believe that we contaminate the purpose of ministry, I believe ministering from that place also produces a spirit of pride, arrogance, and haughtiness. Then we further contaminate not only the induvial, but we contaminate ourselves and the Kingdom of God. That type of ministry is destroying God's people and His reputation. In this lesson, I learned that everyone doesn't see, or understand, things the way that I do. Imagine that!!!!!!!! With that being said, I can't expect people to handle things the way I would, because they may not see things the way that I do, and that is okay. One of the key tools of ministry is to know a person's background, upbringing and then you will understand them a little better. A lot of people are just a product of their environment, but God has the power to take the worst of the worst and turn them into the best of the best. KEEP YOUR MOUTH OFF PEOPLE! Any sinner qualifies for God's grace.

The reason I can't judge the sin that individuals find themselves in is simply because I do not know what that particular person has been through, their background, and neither do I know what they have been taught about the saving grace of forgiveness of Jesus Christ. I don't even know if Jesus has been taught to them at all. This mindset has taught me to overlook the outward actions of a person and to get to the inward issues. The outward actions that you see are just a manifestation of what's going on inside. Now that I understand true ministry, the Holy Spirit has taught me to minister in a way that I can talk to a person and find out the root cause of the outward visible issues. When you find out the root cause of the issue, then you can deal with the real issue. For example, if you are dealing with a person who is addicted to drugs, and you want to see them delivered, telling them to stop using drugs is an option. Providing treatment is helpful, but it's not going to do any good if you don't get to the root cause as to why he or she started using drugs in the first place. Treating the addiction will not do any good if you don't treat the *condition.* That's called cleaning a person up on the outside and neglecting the spirit on the inside. If the person does not get delivered from the root of the addiction, then chances are, he or she is going to start doing drugs all over again. That's why it is imperative that we get to the root of the issue and seek God as to how He wants us to minister to it.

I understand now that God even placed me at my job to help develop certain ministry skills. Lord help me! I work for a huge billing company that deals with billing and collections. This job that I can't stand has taught me some of the most valuable and necessary things for ministry. It has equipped me with skills that I did not have. I can honestly say that this job has helped prepare me for Kingdom work. I bet you ask, how? Ha! Listen, it sounds funny, but it's the truth. In this job, you learn to listen to people with your heart, and you learn to pay attention to details, and what they are saying. You get people calling in yelling at you every day, and you can't yell back, or talk crazy back to them. You must reply to the people very calmly, nicely, and professionally. After you do that for several years this type of calmness becomes who you are, and it gets to the point where people can say or do things to you, and it doesn't even phase you. I am not saying that it keeps you mellow all the time, but it does for about ninety percent of the time. This job broke me from being so bitter, mean, negative and stubborn. I had to learn to talk to people, instead of talking at them. I never knew this was an issue until I listened to myself on a recording. I thought, "Oh, Jesus! Now I got to change my whole tone and dialect." I thought, "Is this how I have been talking to people? It's a wonder that I still have friends! JESUS!" I have done this for so long now, that I very rarely get loud, or upset. Ha! I never thought that would be me. That's why I say, "It's all good."

I also meet so many different people that I have to minister to on this job. Every time I want to leave, God sends some more people my way that needs spiritual help. I think to myself, Jesus they are the reason you won't let me leave. Again, when God has us on assignment, we can cry, pout, kick, scream, and do whatever we want, but at the end of the day, He is going to have His way. We are not going to go anywhere until He releases us.

In the middle of everything else, God also gave me a revelation about my brother's death, and it gave me a peace of mind. I was angry with God for a long time, but He finally revealed to me why He called my brother home (as if he owed me an explanation). He said to me that it was my desire for my brother to be saved. Amidst his heart changing, God said, "I snatched him and brought him home to me. Why? Because he was not spiritually strong enough to stay saved, so rather than risking his soul, I took him. Glory to the highest." Many people may not believe it, but I believe it whole-heartedly. I found a peace of mind in that spiritual explanation.

Currently, I am going through another storm of which I am still waiting for God to show me how it is working for my good. It hurts tremendously, and all I have right now is His Word that "all things work together for the good of them that love the Lord and are called according to His purpose." Again, it's all good. I know I will make it through once again

Prayer for Trusting God Even When We Don't Understand

Father, I come to You as humbly as I know how, asking You, God, to give us a peace of mind even when we don't understand what You are doing. God, you said in your Word that you will keep those in perfect peace whose minds are stayed on you. God, I bind any distractions that have come to cause doubt and confusion. I pray that you instill in us the mind of Christ. Father, I ask that you give us the grace of wisdom to know that we may never understand, or we may never figure everything out, and it is well with our soul. God, we ask that you strengthen us to trust you. Father, we take authority over every spirit of doubt, fear, and unbelief. God, sometimes the "not knowing" will send us into a mind of confusion, but God we are casting all of our fears and concerns on you. Father, I ask that you give us that sweet rest in you. Father, you said in your Word that you did not give us the spirit of fear, but that of power and of a sound mind. You also said you are not the author of confusion, but that of peace. So, God, we are seeking you for peace, power and a sound mind, and we declare that is so, in Jesus' name. Amen!

Chapter 11

Nevertheless – Not My Will but Thy Will be Done

"For we know in part, and we prophesy in part. But when that which is perfect is come, then that which is in part shall be done away." (1 Corinthians 13: 9-10)

I was not ready for this next tragedy. Just when you think that you see a small light at the end of the tunnel, here comes another blow. Someone I trusted and loved dearly hurt me to the core of my heart. However, there was a storm before the storm. I don't think it was the storm itself is what damaged me, but the spiritual and mental rollercoaster that it took me on is what caused the most damage.

I was pregnant and was making plans to get married. I was thinking, Hallelujah! God has finally come through for me. It was probably the most exciting time of my life because I was finally pregnant at forty-two years old. I was so happy and excited. Well, needless to say, the thrill didn't last long. The sense of excitement left me quickly.

Everything was going well, but my spirit was somehow not resting, so I went for my first ultrasound. I received the most devastating news. "You are going to miscarry." Here I go again. You know my routine by now, I am not receiving anything the doctors are telling me. At that time, I started praying and rebuking, fasting and speaking life over my womb. I found every scripture that dealt with life, or breath and I declared it over my life and over my womb.

I was praying non-stop for God to breathe life into my womb and save my baby. I reached out to every prayer group that I knew and had them praying for me. I was begging God not to take my child. This was my first pregnancy, and I just knew that God was going to allow my child to live. The Bible says that if I declare and decree a thing, then it shall be established.

I declared and decreed life until I couldn't think straight. Then the unthinkable happened……the blood came, and it was not the blood of Jesus! I started having pain like I had never experienced. I was in so much pain, physically, emotionally, and spiritually, but I didn't want to bother anyone, so I drove myself to the hospital. I could barely set up straight due to the pain in my abdomen. I couldn't see the road clearly because of the tears that were coming out of my eyes. It was a complete catastrophe. I remember lying in the hospital bed still believing God because no situation is too much for Him right? I chose to believe the report of the Lord that my baby shall live and not die.

Well, I lost my baby. What a spiritual blow! At that point, I didn't know what to do. I did not want to minister. The man that I was supposed to marry slowly fell off. He was nowhere around as I was going through that turmoil, so what once caused me so much joy, had now become the worst pain in my life. Oh yes, I decided that I was over this God "thing" because once again, I worked the Word of God in my life and it still didn't work. As a believer, all we have been taught is to put the Word of God on it, and whatever we ask, it shall come to pass. Well, I did just that, and nothing happened. I was over it. Well, let me re-phrase that. Something did happen, it was just not what I wanted to happen.

During that time of loss, I suffered tremendously. I went into hiding and did not come out of my house. I cut off contact with just about everyone. I just wanted to be alone. I wanted to go somewhere and die. I thought, God, you allowed my dreams and hopes to get up, and you immediately came and stripped me of everything, just that quick. God, you are supposed to love me, after all, that is what your Word teaches. The truth is, this feels like you hate me.

I was crying and asking God, "Why do you hate me so much? Why will you not give me a *yes* to any of my prayers? Are you even there?" I told Him, "I am so numb to life that I don't care if I live or if I die. God, I don't care about you. I don't care about ministry. I don't care about nothing right now." Again, I refused to preach about a God that did not love me. I refused to preach a gospel that did not work for me. I wasn't doing it anymore.

I remember going to sing at a church program that I had accepted before the miscarriage. No matter what, I always tried and honor my word. I was tearing up while trying to sing an old spiritual song called **By the Grace**. I had no spirit in me, or no unction of the Holy Ghost should I say. I was just a shell up there singing. My heart was so far from God, and the truth is I didn't want to be there.

I was at a point in my life where my spirit had gotten tired. I had literally become weary and drained. I had no more fight left in me, and I was not trying to get any either. I prayed and asked God to take my life, but I said, "I don't want it to hurt. I prefer to die in my sleep. This journey that has been assigned to me is just too much for me to handle." I wanted to die, I so wanted to go and be with my parents, my brother and my son. Somehow or another I know that my child was a boy. You would think that I wanted to be with Jesus, but at that time.... Jesus? Nah, I was good.

Honestly, I know that God must have had His hand on me because to this day, I still don't know how I made it through that tragedy. This was one of the worst experiences that I had ever had, and you know just by reading this book that I have been through some absolutely terrible tragedies. I do know that I have not gotten over the loss of my son because as I sit here writing about my loss, the tears are still flowing down my face because this is a very emotional subject for me. Even though I would not acknowledge it, and even though I did not feel it, but all I had at that time was God.

I still don't understand why He said "No" to my prayers and took my son, but I still trust Him. I still believe that He knows what is best for me and He does not make mistakes. The truth is, I really don't have a choice but to trust Him. Even if I decide not to trust Him, it is not going to bring my son back. Not trusting

God, is not going to change the situation into what I want it to be.

Let me be clear. It was not the storm itself that broke me, but it was that joyous moment I experienced for the first time ever in my life, and it was quickly shattered. It broke my faith, it broke my spirit, it broke my belief system, it broke my prayer life, it broke my social life, it broke my ministry life, it broke my womanhood, it broke everything about me.

I believed in something that did not work for me. With that situation, I can honestly say that I had to be like Job and say, "Though He slay me, yet will I trust Him." Still, I never pretended like everything was okay. I told God how I felt, and I told Him my truths. I stayed away from everyone. I know my family did not understand what was going on, but I just could not deal with people at that time. Also, with this type of loss brings a sense of embarrassment. A forty-one-year-old woman that has no kids, and could not carry one, that was embarrassing. Then I had to think, do I want to hear the apologies, and the theories, and the *why comes*? Nope, so it was easier for me to stay away from people and Jesus. I told God that nothing in life is worth me getting excited over because no sooner than I get excited you come and take it. I know that is a terrible way to live as a believer, but my track record says it is understandable.

I experienced a lot of pain with my fiancé at the time, but I allowed that **pain** to push me into my **purpose**. I don't really want to elaborate a lot on him because he and I are still good friends. It is very ironic, because in the earlier part of the year before hell broke loose, I named my women's conference, "From Pain to Purpose," and I scheduled it for the month of October. Obviously, God already knew what I was going to face moving forward. All this pain came right before my first women's conference. I believe that God allowed the storm to test me, to see if I would go through with the conference, or if I was going to cancel it.

While I was in my pain and hurt, I did think about canceling the conference, and then God said, "You could cancel the conference if it was YOUR conference, but since the conference is mine, you cannot cancel." So, I had to go on several spiritual fasts. I had to cry countless tears. I had to study my Word almost non-stop because now, I need to take authority over my flesh, will, and over my emotions. But, when my flesh lined up with my spirit, and my spirit lined up with the Word of God, canceling the conference was not an option.

Sometimes we have understood the scripture in Luke 9:23 "And He said to them all, if any man will come after me, let him deny himself, and take up his cross daily, and follow me." We need to understand that when we say "Yes" to God, we will be tested. There is no other way around it. Saying yes to God initially means that I throw the very essence of my being into is His being. When we do this, you invite God into your life to do as He pleases. Ultimately the goal is for Him to come in and make you into what He wants you to be. This means that your life will more than likely get worse before it gets better, but if you stay faithful, He will give you a life-changing experience. It's almost like you say here God, here are the broken pieces of my life and of my heart. Fix it! We all know that when things are being fixed, there may be some re-arranging that takes place, as well as we may have to get rid of some things for the *fixing* to be complete. It will get hard, but you must continue to pray. Prayer becomes the tool to keep you and your mind in Gods perfect will. When I said, "Yes God, I will do the women's conferences," He said, "Okay, I need to reveal your true motives for the conferences, what is your true intent. Is it about me, or is it about you trying to be seen?"

He allowed heartaches and disasters to come along before the date of the event, just to see if He could trust me to carry out the assignment. You see, saying, "Yes," to God is not a fight, but *keeping* your "Yes" to God is where the fight comes in. You've got to fight for your "Yes!" Jesus said, "Let him deny himself, take up his cross and follow me." He gave three different commands that we must do, in order for our "Yes" to be accepted into the Kingdom. According to this scripture, you can't even begin to follow Him, until you deny yourself. It is not by coincident that denying yourself, is the first thing that you must do. If you can't deny yourself, then you sure won't be able to take up a cross or carry a cross, and without a cross, you cannot follow Jesus. As my grandmother used to say, "No cross, no crown!"

This is what is wrong with many church folks. We say, "Yes" with our lips, but our actions say, "No." I could have easily given into what my flesh wanted, which was to say, "Women's Conference Cancelled" and went on about my life. But, I knew that God's people needed to be delivered, and I had to *man up* and say, "Nevertheless, not my will but God your will be done."

After saying, "Yes" to God, this scripture will become a default setting because true believers will find themselves quoting it for the rest of their lives. Why, because it's all about denying our flesh and doing what pleases the Master, and not what pleases the flesh. Contrary to what church folks say, we cannot serve God and the flesh, we have got to choose one. Sin will feel good to the flesh because, according to the Apostle Paul, "there is nothing good that comes from the flesh", so therefore sin feels comfortable to our flesh. It is only in the consistency of denying the flesh for the will of God, will flesh become uncomfortable to sin. This is the time where most people fall off because we do not want to deny the flesh for the will of God, and fight. We want it to come easy. This is the human side of us, and it is definitely an understandable side, but God did not promise us that living for Him would be easy. We have been given clear and specific instructions from Jesus Christ himself, "If any man will come after me, let him deny himself, and take up his cross and follow me," Luke 9:23.

I find it interesting that in the depths of the pain is where I discovered that I was still carrying the weight of some of the old burdens. God revealed to me that I was still carrying the weight of my childhood scars. I didn't even know they were there until He gave me the spiritual insight. During this period, I was seeking the face of God like never before. I was seeking to enter His heart and His thoughts. I needed to be near Him, I needed to be overshadowed by His spirit. This was not a situation where I was seeking God because I needed a materialistic blessing. No, this was me seeking God because I was about to lose my whole mind. It was there where God revealed to me the specific burdens that I was still carrying and that it was time to release them. Isn't it amazing how, when you are already going through hurt, that God reveals a deeper issue with you? Maybe that is what my ex-fiancés purpose was in my life, which was to push me to a hurt that was so deep that it opened the door to see a deeper hurt that was already rooted in me. I still sometimes feel as if that was his assignment for my life. I still say that God did not have to take me through all of that. He could have simply just dropped me a note. After the experience that I had, I don't know whether to slap the man that hurt me or tell him, "Thank you." It would probably be a mixture of both. SMILE!

Now here comes the fight. The fight that I did not have in me. The fight that I did not have the strength to fight. I felt like I was having an "outer-body" experience the entire time. Even while walking around doing everyday stuff, I felt like I was in a daze and I really didn't know what to do. At that point, I knew that I had become tired, and weary. My soul was tired of hurting, and my eyes were tired of crying. I was tired of seeking God, I was over it. All I knew is that I wanted my spirit to be free of my ex-fiancé, to be free of my past, to be free of the loss of my brother, to be free of the loss of my child, to be free of the pain of my divorce. I just wanted to be free. After all, whom the Son has set free is free indeed, right? Yes, that is a true statement, but what we often don't realize is that becoming free means that the things that have us in bondage has to come off from us, voluntarily or involuntarily.

At that time, I didn't care. I wanted all of the chains and

bondages to let me go. So I said, "God, whatever you need to do to heal me, do it, even if it hurts me more. I need you to heal me." I figured, while I was in the travailing classroom of hurt and pain, I might as well come out of it as pure gold. "I'm already here. I might as well allow God to completely cleanse and purge me. Yep, ouch!"

In life, there are choices that we must make. We can choose to be mad at God and angry at the world. We can choose to live in the past pain or forgive. We can choose to be delivered or blame others for our failures. We can choose to blame others as to why we don't have anything or to turn to alcohol and drugs, or we can choose to turn back to Jesus! No matter what we do, it's always a choice, and it's all a choice that *we* make. I figured that whether I am with Christ or not, hurt is going to happen. Trouble is going to come whether you are saved or a sinner, so I decided that if I was going to hurt, I might as well go through the hurt with Jesus.

My thoughts were mostly, how was I going to get back whole? What could I do from this broken place? I knew that I had to start moving. I knew that I could not heal by staying in the place that was killing me. The problem was, in my spirit I wanted to move, but in my flesh, I wanted to have a pity party. I had to lay there for a couple of days until I convinced myself to move. Just like a baby, I started by scooting just a bit, and then I literally had to crawl back to my faith. The crawl was slow and painful but sure. Listen, it doesn't matter how you get back to our faith, as long as you get there. Crawling is a slow process, but at least there is movement. You must be moving. Yes, it will seem as though you're at the very bottom of your life, and that you are in the lowest of low positions, and you probably are. The main thing is, no matter how low you are, you need to make sure you are constantly moving - even if you must start out by scooting.

The truth of the matter is, we can allow the pain to make us better, or make us bitter. Those are our only two choices in the matter. We can set our minds to believe whatever it is that we want to believe, but still, we only have two choices. I chose to allow it to make me better. I slowly began to pray.

If you have ever prayed while you are in pain, it is a heck of an experience. It takes strong willpower to pray from a broken place. The worst thing that we can do is say, "I don't feel like praying," and then don't pray. Listen, this thing is not based on how we feel but based on what the Word of God says. How can we hear God if we are not communicating with Him? Yes, we must communicate with Him from that broken place. I kept reading Psalms 27 (two to three times) per day. God spoke to me through the pain to let me know that there were things in my life that I needed to change. When God speaks to us, His instructions will help us to learn and grow. We must keep in mind that we are in pain which puts us in a vulnerable place. This is the place where the enemy will come in and whisper all type of things that will attempt to draw us away from God.

The enemy is often able to deceive us because when he comes, he comes in a calm way, and with the truth, but it is a truth that he has manipulated. He deceived Eve by presenting her with the truth. Just like Eve, we fall prey to the deceit and the lies of the enemy. Once we open ourselves up to communicating with the devil, especially while in a broken place, we set ourselves up to be destroyed. I knew that it would be easy for me to succumb to the words of the enemy because I was already blaming God for everything. So there I was fighting again. I was fighting for my mind, my peace, and my self-worth. I knew that the most critical thing for me to do was to protect my spirit man. I had to protect myself from anything that had the potential to cause me to pull away from God. It is a dangerous place to confuse madness with strength. When we are mad or angry, we tend to team up with the devil and accept his tactics, and his truths (lies). I knew that I was angry with God, so I hardly left my house. I really did not speak to anyone, and I did not let anyone speak to me. The only person that I communicated with was the Holy Spirit. It's kind of like being mad at your spouse, but he is the only person that you would talk to, although he is the one that caused the hurt. I made a choice to go through my storms with Jesus Christ.

I remember when I was talking to one of my sisters. I said, "I am reading Psalms 27 every day." She said, "My question is, 'Is it ministering to you yet?'" I said, "Nope, but imma keep reading until it does." So many times, we expect a quick fix. If healing does not come within a certain amount of time, then we quit believing, we quit reading the Word of God and then we lose the will to pray. We basically give up and have nothing of God going into our spirits, when He specifically stated in His Word that we are to renew our minds, daily. That instruction was given to us without condition. When we cut off the Holy Spirit or we stop Him from operating in our lives, we then become an open target for the enemy to begin to manipulate our thinking. When we were on the streets and wanted something, we would not stop until we got it, no matter how long it took even if we had to fight someone. It is imperative that we keep that same mentality in the spiritual. I had made up in my mind that I was not going to let God go until He came and restored me. If He did not manifest himself on Monday, then I had it in my mind that I was going to get right back on the floor, lay on my face and seek Him on Tuesday. I was determined to do whatever I had to do so that I could come out of this situation victorious, even if it meant staying stretched out on the floor. I have learned that my outcome depended on how strong my will was to overcome the obstacle.

Just as Jacob wrestled with the angel, sometimes we are going to have to wrestle too. In Genesis 32:24, the Bible says, "So Jacob was left alone, and a man wrestled with him till daybreak. When the man saw that he could not overpower him, he touched the socket of Jacobs's hip so that his hip was wrenched as he wrestled with the man." The man touched the socket of Jacobs's leg, and it crippled him, but that did not stop Jacob from wrestling. Jacob understood who he was wrestling with, and knew that the blessing was connected to this fight. My God! Although Jacob was in pain, he stayed in the fight. He had made up in his mind that he was not letting go of that fight because the fight had something that he both wanted and needed. That is just like the fight that we are in. The enemy tries to make us feel that we are so hurt, and fragile, that we can't fight, or maybe even the fight is useless. But, I declare to every reader that God has something in the fight that you need, and the enemy doesn't want you to discover what it is. We might not be able to see it or feel it because of the pain but know that God does not waste a *valley experience.* Giving up is not an option because giving up only leads back to square one, and once there we will discover that the situation has only gotten worse.

Let me share a secret. Those who have been chosen by God will see this same test again, so just go ahead and pass it now. Ask God, "How do I handle this hurt? I want to handle it right because I don't want to bring shame to the Kingdom in any way." Many times, when we are hurting, God allows us to be on display. Just as He did the Hebrew boys when they were thrown into the furnace. God put them on display so that people could see their actions while they were in the fire. That is why, we must be careful how we react to pain, hurt, and betrayal. I remember praying and telling God that I was not in a good place spiritually, but I wanted to make sure that I represented the Kingdom correctly, even while hurting. I literally prayed and asked God to keep people out of my path, and what do you think happened? Yep, people were coming from the north, east, south, and west! I, Linda, did not want to be bothered, but I put a smile on my face and began to shine for the King. Again, you don't have to *feel* like shining, to shine.

I figured that since I was already hurting, I might as well go ahead and capitalize off this pain. I told the Lord that since I was already hurting, any other hurt, pain, un-forgiveness, bitterness, resentment, or weight that I was carrying that I was not aware of, to please reveal it to me so I can give it to Him. I was on my face crying out to the Lord. I told Him that I was going to be like Jacob in a sense, that I was not going to let Him go until He healed and restored me. One morning I told God, "I've got to go to work, but when I get off, I will be right back here on my face seeking you because I can't go any further until you mend my broken heart." I did that for about a month, if not longer. We have to be determined that we are going to come out of our intense situations victoriously, and we will not accept anything less.

All I can say is that God showed up in my life in a mighty way. Not only did He heal me, but He gave me my joy and my shout back. He gave me a new walk and a new talk. He put a new song in my heart. (I feel like preaching now.) He gave me more ministry tools to help deliver His people.

In life, things will happen that we don't understand, but it's okay. Do I fully understand why God did not allow my baby to live? No, I don't. Was I wrong to be angry? In my heart, I don't feel like I was wrong. Even when Jesus was on the cross, He asked God, "Why hast thou forsaken me?" Too many times we as children of God try and mask the pain we are suffering. Maybe we are trying to do what the book of James teaches us - to count it all joy when we encounter temptation, James 1:2,3. When we are suffering and acknowledge that the suffering hurts, we feel guilty. Why? Because the pain is unbearable, and we cannot count it all joy right now. Then we feel as though we have let God down. Keep this in mind, when Jesus went to the cross, He did not go laughing, joyous, clapping His hands, or screaming, "COULD YOU HURRY UP AND TAKE ME TO THE CROSS?" No! He went in agony, but the main thing is *He went!* If you are going through agony, and you feel like crying instead of clapping, go ahead and cry. Just because you cry instead of rejoicing, does not mean you don't have any faith or you are not saved. Don't let church folks tell you that you are not saved, or you don't have faith because you cried. As a matter of fact, keep them out of your ear and out of your business. It is okay to cry, but after you cry, get up and get back into the spiritual fight. You may have to join forces with some warriors to pray and push you through, and that is also okay just as long as you get through.

As the Apostle Paul said, "I may not know everything, and I may not understand everything, but what I do know is, I press towards the mark of the high calling which is in Christ Jesus." Don't miss the most important word of that scripture, *press*. Even the Apostle Paul had to *press*, so that lets me know that there are going to be certain things in life that hit us so hard, that we are going to have to *Press*......Somebody shout *PRESS!!!* What I do know about God is, no matter what He allows in my life, I trust Him. The Bible teaches us that we learn in part, we understand in part, and we prophesy in part. We will do this until the day our Lord and our Savior makes His return. Then we will understand everything in full. Until then, I just trust God.

Prayer for miscarriages

Father, God, I am petitioning the throne of grace on behalf of the couples who have miscarried or lost a child. Father, the pain is so deep that only you can get to it. The pain is so deep that only the spirit of the Holy Ghost can penetrate through the layers of our soul. Your holy spirit is the only one that can get to the very bone marrow of our being. I ask that you heal the hearts of the one who carried the child. Father, you know the pain that we have experienced because you too, lost your son Jesus Christ. Father, you already know the spiritual paralysis that the pain causes, and what we feel. Father, I ask that you come and heal the heart, heal the emotions, heal our thoughts. Father, I ask that in the name of Jesus that you hear our hearts cry. This pain is like no other pain, and your strength is the only thing that can get us through it.

Father, I petition the throne of Grace on behalf of those who cannot pray right now because of the impact of the pain, that you accept my prayer on their behalf, and that you send your ministering angels to come and hold and comfort them. Father, I ask that as they cry themselves to sleep that you would hold them and their family's right in the cradle of your arms. Father, don't let them go until you have healed their hearts, delivered their pain, and restored their minds. Father, you said in your Word that you would give us beauty for ashes, so God, again, we are standing on your Word and trusting you to intervene and heal the broken hearts. God, we love you, and we trust that you don't make any mistakes. Father, I ask that you give us the grace to accept this loss, and to strengthen us to carry on in your name. We ask these, and blessings, in Jesus' name, Amen!

Battle Behind the Sword

Chapter Twelve
Picking up the Pieces of my Heart

"He healeth the brokenhearted, and bindeth up their wounds" (Psalm 147:3).

The only way to push and pick up the broken pieces of your life is through Jesus Christ. Philippians 4:13 says, "I can do all things through Christ which strengthened me." There is no other way to complete healing, except through Him. When we try to heal through any other way, it becomes a situation where we are not healed, but we have masked the pain. If we're are not careful we will believe that we are healed, and the truth is, we just moved on. We learned to cope with the pain, but God wants to heal us whole-heartedly, and completely. Yes, it takes time for complete healing to take place, but it is time well spent. Psalms 147:3 says, "He healeth the brokenhearted, and bindeth up their wounds."

This can only happen if we allow God into the darkest, deepest, and most secret place in our hearts.

One of the main reasons for writing this book is to acknowledge my pain, my struggles, and my truths. Just like in the Bible, when the spies went to go seek out the land, they acknowledged that the giants were there. They came back and reported to Moses that there were giants in the land. They acknowledged the giants were there, but they also acknowledged God in His strength. Caleb understood that if God is for them, the giants will appear as grasshoppers when compared to God. Just like Caleb, we must acknowledge our struggles, but we must also acknowledge that God is greater than any struggle that we may face. The trick is giving the struggle to Him so that He can heal us. Whatever we do, we must remember not to get lost in the struggle that we forget to give the struggle to God.

I have grown to learn, that the only way that true healing can take place is when we understand and accept our reality. I have accepted the sufferings that I have encountered. Did it hurt? Yes, but is it the end of the world? Nope. It is only the end of the world if I allow it to be. Don't allow the disappointments of life to stop you from living and enjoying life.

As children of God, we must continue to live and enjoy our lives, by simply knowing that we are secure in Him. By simply knowing that our life is in His hands. God has given me a circle of women with whom I can laugh, and cry with. One thing that I do know about these ladies is that they will never manipulate, betray or deceive me. How do I know this? It's called discernment. As I stated earlier, the more trials we endure, the sharper our discernment will be. These ladies are not gossipers, they just don't talk about people, but they are truly about God's business and taking care of the Kingdom. So, word to the wise, if your friends gossip about other people to you, then chances are they are gossiping about you to other people. *Don't share any of your struggles with them.* We must learn to take our issues to the throne of grace until God sends some true warriors who can support us in our challenges.

Don't just lay there in your room with the blinds down, in the dark. Darkness is the enemy's playground. After a storm has hit, if you've just got to lay around for a while, that is totally understandable. However, open the blinds and lay around with the sun coming through the windows.

Also, turn the TV on to a gospel channel of your choice. Let your flesh and spirit soak up that Word. The environment in which we heal in has everything to do with the healing process and the outcome. When you are in that place where depression is knocking at the door and it's about to tear it down, the last thing that you want to do is be around people that are depressed, or full of negativity. Check your environment and check your surroundings. What kinds of dark spirits have you allowed into your atmosphere where healing is trying to dwell. What is your healing environment like? Is there a suppressed spirit that prevents healing from taking place? Is the WORD going out? Is worship going out? Once again, check the place that you are trying to heal in.

I know this one sounds a little strange, especially to the church folk who have everything figured out, but make sure to find a trustworthy Kingdom vessel individual to whom you can vent to. You need someone that you can let your hair down and just let it all out; the good, the bad and the ugly. Just like we do a detox to cleanse our flesh, we need to do a detox to cleanse our spirit. Even if you say some words that are not holy, they will still listen and not judge. We need to get rid of all of the negative emotions that we have pinned up on our inside. Yell, scream, kick - whatever it takes. The truth of the matter is, whatever is in us, that is what is going to come out. The question is, how will it come out?

If we continue to harbor every negative emotion that we encounter, and never release it, then we are setting ourselves up for an explosion that is waiting to happen. When we explode unintentionally, we began to hurt the people that we love. We tend to say and do things that are harmful and hurtful that we really don't mean.

There are some healthy ways to vent and release those negative toxins if you don't want to scream. You can journal or talk to a listening ear. I did all of these, plus I did a lot of venting in the recording studio. Just be sure that you get it out. Personally, I wrote and recorded R&B music that captured my frustration and my hurt.

The biggest mistake that we can make is to become idle and isolate. We don't want to do anything, go anywhere, or talk to anyone. We must find ways to counteract our pain and emotions. For example, if we just came out of a relationship with someone, and we're hurting, the worst thing that we can do is sit around and listen to a song that we enjoyed with that individual. The feelings that we still have will try to pull us back into "what used to be." So listening to that special song is not a good idea because we are trying to come out of "what used to be." That is one of the devil's way of keeping God's people in bondage.

Again, we have to accept that "what used to be" is no more. Then we must make moves to come out of "what used to be." The actions which must be taken are normally going to be the opposite of what we *feel* like doing. For example, people who are hurting may just feel like laying around and crying. However, the best thing to do is get up and get moving. Go outside and enjoy the sunshine; if you have to cry, cry outside in the bright rays of the sun.

Keeping us isolated from spiritual people is another trick of the enemy. Hanging around faith rooted people is where we will get our strength. People who can speak life into us while we are dying is where you want to be, and who you want to speak to regularly. Emotionally, the enemy will try to convince us that we don't need anyone because they are going to laugh at us and make us feel embarrassed. That is just one of his ways of keeping us in bondage to the pain. He does not want us to break free. Trust and believe that when we are in a vulnerable place, he is going to try and capitalize on our sufferings. In order for him to keep a warrior for God down, he will employ every trick that he knows.

When we are vulnerable, our judgment can be a little cloudy. For example, I would say that it was ok for me to be alone because this *felt* like a comfortable and safe place to be. After being alone for a while, we will begin to feel really weighted down because the spirit of the depression will begin to sneak in. Now we are BIG mad because we fell subject to the tricks of the devil. Satan will try to convince us and have us think that faith does not work and that God does not love us.

Look at this way, if the devil is going to convince us that Faith does not work, and we are not strong enough to convince ourselves that it does work, then we need a third voice to come back at him, on our behalf declaring and decreeing the Word of God over our lives. We need someone telling him (Satan) that, "Faith in God does work, and it's because of my faith that God has kept me. It's because of my faith that I have not killed anyone or why I do not have an assault charge. This is how Christians come against the devil. Yes, sometimes we need help to do it, otherwise the conversation is going to be one-sided, and you will eventually begin to believe the word that is being spoken. You literally need someone to argue on your behalf. Remember, that the enemy is also the father of lies, and his mission is to kill, steal and destroy God's people.

The Bible teaches us that when Lazarus died, and Jesus received word that he was dead, He waited. He waited a few days. Jesus did not immediately run to raise Lazarus from the dead. Jesus explained that He did this so people would not be confused and understand that Lazarus was really dead. As a matter fact, Lazarus was so dead that his body had started to stink. In this story, I learned that sometimes God will allow us to encounter dead situations, and He doesn't always run to our defense immediately. He will sometimes wait and allow us to get so low that we can't go any further. That is when He does come to bring us out, and we can make no mistake - it was God who brought us out. It was God who raised up our dead situation. He allows these tests in our lives so that He can get the glory - not the doctor, or the lawyer. If He would have come to Lazarus' aid immediately and raised him up, then some would say that Lazarus was not really dead therefore, there was no miracle performed. But sometimes, God wants to show His power through our dead situations, and sometimes He does not get to us in a hurry. We know that He wants to heal us, raise us up, and restore us, but it must be done in His timing. It's His timing and His way.

As I stated before, healing takes time. At the writing of this book, I am forty-two years old, and I am just now releasing my brother. I just now forgave my mother, and I released every hurt that I was carrying. I told my brother in the spiritual realm that I love him, but I must release him so that I can be about my Father's business.

I've also found that it is in the pain where I found my strength. I found so much spiritual wisdom in the midst of the storm. One thing that is to be understood is some wisdom may be found in the storm, but true wisdom is not understood until after the storm is over. That is when God ties all of the pieces together and makes it all make sense. When we began to pick up the pieces, let's make sure that we are picking up the right pieces for the Master to put them back together again.

It is now that I am walking in my blessed season. It is in this season that I soar like the eagle that God called me to be. It is now that I walk in my purpose, with my head held high, walking straight into my destiny. Everything that God promised me, I'm coming for it. Look out world, because these "high heels" are truly on the move! It is the *pain* that I have endured that has pushed me to this place called "here." If I could encourage someone, I would tell them that God has a purpose and a plan. Sometimes we can't see or understand it because we are blinded by the pain of life. But "stay the course and stay faithful!" God will not let you down. I am a living testimony. Remember, the blessing is in the fight. Ask yourself, how bad do you want it? I don't have to fully understand everything in order to trust God. As a matter of fact, I don't have to understand anything that happens in my life, because I TRUST GOD!

Who is Lady Linda Jenise now? I am new, complete, alive, and free in Christ. I am a fierce and an unstoppable spiritual force to be wrecking with. I have lived so much of life weighted down, but glory to God the weight has been lifted. I can move freely, sing freely, and preach freely. I can now give God everything that is owed to Him, *freely*!

I do not just exist anymore. I live life and I enjoy it. This is the life that Christ died for me to have. I will say this to anyone, "If you are having a problem with trying to discover what your purpose is, look into what you love to do. That may very well be your purpose, and if you don't love to do anything, you can start by picking up trash off the church floor. That may not be your calling or your purpose, but God will direct you to the path that you need to take as long as you are working." The bottom line is, get busy, get moving, get to working and let God order your steps. The Bible says, "Faith without *works*, is dead." Soooo get to working!!

Prayer for Surviving the Storms of Life

Dear heavenly Father, we offer thanks for all that you have done in our lives. We thank you for the hurt. We thank you for the pain, and we thank you for the rain that you allowed in our lives. It is in those storms where we learn to seek you. It is in those storms where we learn to trust you. Although, many of the storms that raged in our lives, we did not and still do not understand, nevertheless somehow, we managed to be strengthened through them. We thank you that we are still here, and still standing on your promise. We thank you for your Word. We thank you that your Word is a strong tower, and the righteous run to it for safety. Father, we understand that even a rose must push through some dirt if it wants to bloom, but it still doesn't change the fact that it is still a rose. And just like the rose, we too must push through some dirt in life if we want to bloom. Father God, we thank you that we are your children and that we have had to push through some dirt, some storms, and some pain, but in spite of it all, we are still here. We were empowered through the pushing. Father, we thank you that you have kept your hand on us. We thank you that you have stayed with us every step of the way.

Father, we bind up every generational curse that has been passed down from generation to generations. We break the curse and we break the powers of the enemy in Jesus' name. We come out of agreement with the curse now in Jesus' name. We declare and decree that Jesus Christ is our Lord and Savior. We bind up the curses, and we send them back to the pits of hell from where they came from. Father, we denounce every spirit of witchcraft that has been spoken over our lives, and we now surrender to Your grace. We now surrender to the wholeness and completeness in You God. We now surrender to the authority of the Holy Ghost. We now surrender to the covering of your son's blood over our lives. Father, we thank you that generational curses are now broken and destroyed. We thank You, Lord, that we no longer have to live in bondage to a curse that we had nothing to do with. Father, we thank you for deliverance. We thank you for chains being broken, and yokes being destroyed. Father, we thank you for the anointing that we can now walk in. We thank you for the warring angels standing charge in our lives.

Father, I cry out on behalf of my sisters, my brothers, and this nation. Father, you have been so merciful to us, and you have kept this nation afloat, but Father, we don't give You your just due praise. This nation does not even recognize, or acknowledge, your existence until tragedy hits. Father, we are a nation that is deliberately approving laws that are in direct contradiction to your Word, and still, expect your blessings to rain down on us. Father, please forgive us for not seeking you, and not worshipping you. Father, those of us who do, God, we ask for your guidance and your instructions. Satan, we declare war on you and your Kingdom. We come in the name of Jesus to take back our young people, to take back our minds, to take back our womanhood and our manhood. We bind up the spirit of homosexuality, the spirit of abuse, the spirit of lack, the spirit of incest, and the spirit of child molestation. Satan, we declare war on you, and we strip you of your devices. We strip you and your imps. We decree and declare the blood of Jesus is against you, and it is more powerful than anything that you have to offer.

Father, I stand in the gap for every man, woman, boy and girl who has been manipulated and deceived by the church, or by anyone who falsely represented your name. Father, I ask that you come in and heal their wounds. Father, I ask that you come in and be a comfort to them and let them know that everyone who represents the Kingdom is not a deceiver. Father, I ask that you teach us who are true and sincere kingdom disciples, how to minister to those who have been hurt by the church. When we meet them Holy Spirit, we ask that you take over. We ask that you give us the words to say that will bring healing to their spirit. Father, I ask that you teach us how to discern who the true and sincere Kingdom disciples are. Teach us how to minister to those who have a stumbling block to those who were truly seeking you, God. Father, give us wisdom on how to get them back. Give us instructions on how to love them. Father, I just thank you for all that you have done. In Jesus' name, Amen!

Excerpts from my Journal
From Pain to Purpose

Pain is a feeling of distress resulting from the stimulation of certain nerve endings, which is caused by suffering or discomfort that is associated with an illness or injury.

Pain is a signal to the body that something is wrong. Without it, we would die from neglecting the pain. Some pain is so severe that it will insist that we stop our daily routine and tend to the need of the pain.

In the spiritual realm, pain will cause us to stop and think, and often it will require us to revisit the reason for the pain. Many times, if we can determine what has caused the pain, then we can seek a resolution to the healing of the pain. Pain, whether it is physical, spiritual, or emotional, should bring the believer closer to God. However, if the pain is not handled correctly, then it can result in negative emotions, such as depression, anxiety, suicidal thoughts, bitterness, etc. The Bible teaches us that we have the power to bring any thought that exalts itself against the knowledge of God into captivity (2 Corinthians 10:5).

The illustration below outlines how pain can push the believer into their Purpose.

P- praying through the pain
U- understanding the pain
R- reacting to the pain
P- power in the pain
O- overcoming the pain
S- strengthened from the pain
E- expecting purpose from the pain

Praying through the Pain

Psalms 34:18

Sometimes the pain is so strong that it paralyzes us and stops all spiritual mobility. Pain can cause us to become immobile, which can help aid in the neglecting of prayer. That is why it is imperative that we do not make our decisions on whether to pray or not to pray, based on feelings and emotions.

Prayer is the most important weapon when dealing with pain. Pray even when you don't feel it's necessary or even if you feel like it's not doing any good. When in prayer, acknowledge your pain. Acknowledge the fact that you understand it's there and you know what it is doing to you. Moreover, as you acknowledge the pain, know that God knows it too and is sitting right beside you, right there, present, powerful, and all loving. God is ready and waiting for you to acknowledge the pain, release it to Him, and leave it with Him.

Understanding the Pain

Proverbs 3:5

If God allows the pain, He will reveal its true and divine purpose. It is hard to understand while you are hurting – it just seems virtually impossible. At this stage, we need to seek God and try not to figure it out. He will reveal its purpose in His timing. It is imperative that we do not focus more on the pain than we do the promise. Understanding the pain simply comes by trusting God and acknowledging Him through the entirety of this season.

God can use the pain to save you, but it is mostly used for others to see His glorious manifestation all while His chosen disciple is dealing with a deep hurt. He wants us to know that it is possible to give Him praise, and glorify Him all while we are hurting in the very depths of our soul. Yes, we may have to fight to get there……… but the key is, just get there.

Reacting to the Pain

1 Peter: 6-7

How you react to pain is probably the most important part of discovering the purpose. When we face painful circumstances or tragedies, we immediately tend to feel sorrow, confusion, anger, and pain. These emotions should push us closer to God. He has clearly stated that He desires that all His children draw closer to Him. So our reactions to pain should push us into a place of worship and seeking God.

Power in the Pain

Romans 8:22

Some people turn away from God during times of pain, which is very easy to do if you choose to soak in it. The battle is turning to God during this time, and oh yes, it is a battle. God wants to strengthen us, and those that trust in the Lord will draw closer to Him by going through the fire and trusting Him by faith. Faith opens up a connection between the healer and the one who desires to be healed.

Those that have been purified by pain can minister to those that are still going through the fire.

- Pain is required for growth (1 Peter 5:10)
- Pain causes you to humble yourself
- Just like a physical birth requires pain, so does a spiritual birth.

God has called us to be His, therefore spiritual growth is a necessity. Yes, it is painful when we are growing, but it is even more painful when you are not growing. This is the time when you must exercise your God-given authority. Remember that Jesus gave us power and authority to put all things under our feet!

Overcoming the Pain

Pain plays a huge part in our lives, and it lets us know that we have been wronged in some type of way - whether physically or emotionally. Pain that is not dealt with will hinder us from moving forward because we tend to become bitter and in a stagnant place. When we have been hurt, wronged or offended, we tend to push away the very thing that we need to help heal us and that is LOVE.

The Bible teaches us that love covers a multitude of faults. Look at how God loves us, the scriptures tell us that He doesn't punish us as our sins deserve. Love gives us the strength to forgive and will release us from transferring your pain from yesterday to today. Love also strengthens, heals, transforms, and ushers us into a purposeful life.

Although difficult, we cannot be afraid of the pain, but rather embrace it, because on the other side of it there is *Purpose*. We cannot get to our purpose if we do not love our way through the pain. Healing can only take place in an environment where love abides.

Strengthened from the Pain

2 Corinthians 12:9-10

God gives us the strength to endure, not to escape. He promised that everything that comes to us, including our pain, is a part of His fatherly love and care. The truth is, He does not promise certain limits to suffering nor does it guarantee personal happiness. God did, however, promise that His strength is made perfect in our weakness. In the pain, God strengthens us to keep us obeying and serving Him, even when we feel tired, overwhelmed, and like we can't go on. It is during these times that He comes in to provide His strength even though sometimes strength is not noticed until after the pain is over.

Expecting the Purpose from the Pain

James 1:5

Our pain will often reveal God's purpose. He can use the pain to save you, but it is mostly used for others so that they can see the deliverance and the glory of God. Be careful how you handle the pain, so that others may be able to see God in you while you are going through the journey. King Nebuchadnezzar would have never seen "the Son of Man" if the Hebrew boys were not forced into the fire (Daniel 3:23).

Your pain often reveals God's purpose for you, God never wastes hurt that He allowed. If you are going through "forced pain", then you should seek God, and ask Him, "Why have you allowed this? What are you trying to teach me?" In time, the purpose will unfold.

End Note

When you make stupid decisions, and it causes pain in your life; you CANNOT blame God for your bad choices. Faith and love are the links to use together in order to experience the healing power of God in the wounded parts of our lives today. Through faith, we can also receive His healing touch in our own woundedness and then pass it on to others around us.

About the Author

Lady Linda Jenise, who with grace, commitment and passion founded the women's ministry *High Heels on the Move Women's Ministry* and *Women of War Kingdom Fellowship*. As God's humble servant, she was licensed and ordained as a minister of the Gospel of Jesus Christ in 2007. She currently resides in Columbia MO, where she obtained a bachelor's degree in Business Administration from Columbia College. Her passion is to always be a willing and available vessel for God and to minister the gospel as the Holy Spirit leads. With a powerful testimony, she has dedicated her life to be a reflection of God's grace and wisdom.

Contact Information: lglispie@hotmail.com

Lady Linda Jenise

TO PUBLISH YOUR

STORY OR BOOK

CONTACT

WILLIAMS & KING PUBLISHERS

888-645-0550

INFO@WILLIAMSANDKINGPUBLISHERS.COM

OR

TO LEARN ABOUT

OTHER BOOKS PUBLISHED

BY

WILLIAMS AND KING PUBLISHERS

VISIT

WILLIAMSANDKINGPUBLISHERS.COM